FACT, VALUE, AND GOD

Fact, Value, and God

Arthur F. Holmes

WILLIAM B. EERDMANS PUBLISHING COMPANY
GRAND RAPIDS, MICHIGAN

Wm. B. Eerdmans Publishing Co.
255 Jefferson Ave. S.E., Grand Rapids, Michigan 49503 /
P.O. Box 163, Cambridge CB3 9PU U.K.

Printed in the United States of America

02 01 00 99 98 97   7 6 5 4 3 2 1

Library of Congress Cataloging-in-Publication Data

Holmes, Arthur Frank, 1924- .
Fact, value, and God / Arthur F. Holmes.
p.   cm.
Includes bibliographical references.
ISBN 0-8028-4312-3 (paper : alk. paper)
1. Facts (Philosophy) 2. Values. 3. Philosophy.
4. God. I. Title
B105.F3H65   1997
171 — dc21   97-6257
CIP

www.eerdmans.com

Contents

CONTENTS

Preface

TWENTIETH-CENTURY MORAL PHILOSOPHY has had a checkered career.
First of all, normative questions about human actions were sidetracked
by metaethical questions about the meaning of words like "good" and
"right." Then, deontological and teleological theories competed for an
emerging market in "applied ethics." Virtue ethics then challenged the
"applied ethics" monopoly, while Alasdair MacIntyre made the existence of rival moral traditions philosophically respectable. Meanwhile
Richard Rorty declared this a post-metaphysical culture: the claim that
truth is somehow objective, "out there," is the unusable legacy of an
age that saw the world as created by God. Historicism, Rorty claimed,
frees us from theology and metaphysics and unchanging truth.[1]

This book began as an attempt to explore historical ways of
grounding moral values objectively in the nature of reality. Unconvinced that we live in a value-free universe, that fact and value are
ultimately unrelated, or that we have to create all our own values rather
than discovering the good, I wanted to explore the fact-value connection
in the larger context of metaphysical and theological views. What
emerged is a more pervasive linkage than I had anticipated between
religious and moral beliefs. Rorty is in measure right. But the claim
that values are somehow objective, "out there," is the legacy on which
we still need to draw.

In the Judeo-Christian tradition, of course, concepts of moral law,

---

1. *Contingency, Irony and Solidarity* (Cambridge Univ. Press, 1989), intro.
and ch. 1.

sin, and righteousness assume the reality of objective and universal moral norms. So too does the Christian gospel, with its belief in an ordered creation whose promise will be fulfilled in the *eschaton*. But the history of philosophy is religiously diverse. Concepts of God differ: Plato's Form of the Good, Aristotle's Unmoved Mover, the divine Logos, the First Cause, Hegel's Absolute, and so forth. And philosophical frameworks differ: different cosmologies, different theories of universals, different ethical theories, different epistemologies. In all this diversity, are there any apparent general trends on the relation of the fact-value issue to God?

In the present study, the early Greek idea of cosmic justice is seen leading to metaphysical accounts of cosmic order and so to the medieval vision of a creation ordered by the divine Logos (Chapters 1 to 6). With the rise of nominalism, the confluence of God's will and right reason points to the image of God in human nature, giving rise in turn to confidence in the moral psychology we were divinely endowed with (Chapters 7 to 10). Kant and Hegel (Chapters 10 and 11) return to the idea of a divinely sustained cosmic moral order. While Mill's utilitarianism (Chapter 12) cannot altogether escape the imaginative appeal of Jesus, Nietzsche declares the death of God in order (Chapter 13) to "transvalue" traditional Judeo-Christian values. The relation of theological facts to moral values is inescapable, unless the existence of theological facts is denied.

Plainly this work is selective. I have chosen to look primarily at key figures who emphasized different aspects of the subject and whose distinctive ideas contributed to the unfolding story. I have gone as far as Mill and Nietzsche in order to introduce the empiricist and noncognitive bases for ethics that dominate the twentieth century, in place of the previous metaphysical and theological foundations. Moreover, I assume that readers will already have a general knowledge of the philosophers discussed.

I am indebted to Mark Talbot's perceptive reading of the manuscript, to Catherine Blackford's excellent work putting it all on disc, and to my patient wife Alice for many years of loving encouragement.

CHAPTER ONE

Cosmic Justice and the Pre-Socratics

WESTERN PHILOSOPHY first emerged six hundred years before Christ in Greek cities on the shores of the Aegean Sea. At least three different emphases may be found in historical accounts of these Pre-Socratic philosophers, the most common being that they replaced the early mythology about nature and the gods with a more scientific outlook. While this emphasis figures large in accounts of both Greek science and Greek philosophy, it suggests that the main and perhaps only philosophical contribution of the Pre-Socratics was their cosmological speculation, which prepared the way for Platonic and Aristotelian science and metaphysics. Aristotle himself may have started this reading of their work in book one of his *Metaphysics*, where he surveys their anticipations of his own kind of causal explanation. But doubtless it has been reinforced by the scientific mentality, which tends to measure past thinkers by comparison with the modern scientific outlook rather than reading them on their own terms. And since the modern scientific outlook views nature as impersonal and value-free, it tends to ignore "naive" views to the contrary.[1]

---

1. This scientific emphasis is evident in such classics as W. T. Stace, *A Critical History of Greek Philosophy* (Macmillan, 1920); Frank Thilly, *A History of Philosophy*, rev. by Ledger Wood, 3rd ed. (Holt, Rinehart and Winston, 1951); W. Windelband, *A History of Philosophy* (first published 1901; Harper Torchbooks, 1958); E. Zeller, *Outline of the History of Greek Philosophy*, 13th

1

A second emphasis goes back at least to Cicero's *On the Nature of the Gods,* which surveys emerging conceptions of a divine intelligence behind the cosmic order. The Pre-Socratics then appear to prepare the way for Plato's theology and beyond. Some early church fathers like Justin Martyr and Clement of Alexandria go even further, seeing them as a providential preparation for the Christian gospel.[2]

While past history undoubtedly prepares the ground for what comes later, and while the Pre-Socratics made major contributions to both the science and the theology of the ancients, these contributions by no means exhaust their significance. Nor does this approach necessarily read them on their own terms, in the context of their own cultural roots. A third emphasis, in fact, is closer to their own intentions and stresses their continuity with the past — more specifically with the idea of a law-governed universe. Their very attempts to explain the ordered processes of nature relate to the growing ethical conviction, entrenched in their cultural heritage, that values are rooted in reality.[3] This third emphasis rejects the assumption that nature is value-free, and it implies that the god of these philosophers is likely to be an intelligence behind the moral order as well as the physical order that we observe.

In early Greek mythology, no divine intelligence gives nature either harmony or direction, for nature and human life are ultimately governed not by gods or god but by an impersonal fate or destiny, *Moira.* On the

---

ed. (Humanities, 1931); as well as in recent textbooks by G. L. Abernathy and T. A. Langford, *Introduction to Western Philosophy* (Dickenson, 1970); Wallace Matson, *A New History of Philosophy* (Harcourt Brace Jovanovich, 1987); and Samuel Stumpf, *Socrates to Sartre,* 4th ed. (McGraw-Hill, 1988). Frederick Copleston also emphasizes the scientific, but notes briefly that earlier conceptions of law were extended by the Pre-Socratics to the entire cosmos. See *A History of Philosophy* (Newman, 1960), vol. 1, pp. 14, 25.

2. See especially Werner Jaeger, *The Theology of the Early Greek Philosophers* (Clarendon, 1947); Richard Kroner, *Speculation in Pre-Christian Philosophy* (Westminster, 1956); and Diogenes Allen, *Philosophy for Understanding Theology* (John Knox, 1985).

3. See especially Werner Jaeger, *Paideia* (Oxford Univ. Press, 1939); F. M. Cornford, *From Religion to Philosophy* (first published 1912; Harper Torchbooks, 1957); Terence Irwin, *Classical Thought* (Oxford Univ. Press, 1989). See also the discussion of Homer's ethic in Alasdair MacIntyre, *Whose Justice? Which Rationality?* (Univ. of Notre Dame Press, 1988), chs. 2 and 3; and an older article by Gregory Vlastos, "Equality and Justice in Early Greek Cosmologies," *Classical Philosophy* 42 (1947): 156-78.

one hand, Homer's gods are limited, each to his or her own province: some are inherently fickle, some are intelligent, and some are even concerned with justice. Zeus is more in control of things than the others, but even his control is limited. On the other hand, human action has its roots in how one's nature or character responds to circumstances, so that heroic qualities and actions are largely outside one's control. Born into a good family, endowed with beauty, wealth, and status, one's honor governs what one does; but honor ignores the concerns of society, the needs of others, and even one's own self-interest. In the *Iliad* the fated Achilles could not really help himself, and the prospects for justice are precarious. Zeus punishes the Trojans, to be sure, yet victorious Odysseus strives in vain to return home, while false friends devour his resources and court his grieving wife.

In the *Odyssey*, prospects improve because the gods take more interest, and heroic virtues are no longer to the fore. With Zeus's support, Athena rallies to the side of Odysseus's son and helps secure justice at last. Justice is no mere social convention, but is the expected natural outcome.

Hesiod goes further. In the *Theogony* it is Zeus who dispenses to the other gods those provinces that *Moira* had previously assigned. Zeus's daughter *Dike,* the goddess of justice, oversees the actions of mortals and is respected by all the gods of Olympus. Hesiod's *Works and Days* calls humans from violence, bribery, and crooked decisions to justice and honest labor. The person who does evil to another does evil to himself, for in the end justice wins. In Hesiod, justice has become part of the cosmic order:

> Listen to justice, and put away all notions of violence. Here is the law, as Zeus established it for human beings; as for fish, and wild animals, and the flying birds, they feed on each other, since there is no idea of justice among them; but to men he gave justice, and she in the end is proved the best thing they have.[4]

This reflects a concept of justice characteristic of a Greek city-state governed not by arbitrary aristocrats but by a community of equals in open debate. Such a law-governed society becomes a microcosm of nature as a whole.

Aeschylus's *Oresteia* is even more explicit, for the drama of the house

---

4. Hesiod's *Works and Days,* trans. R. Lattimore (Univ. of Michigan Press, 1959), ll. 276-79.

of Atreus is about heavenly and human justice. Agamemnon, having sacrificed his daughter to the gods while seeking revenge against Troy, is murdered by his wife Clytemnestra and succeeded on the throne by her lover Aegisthus. When Agamemnon's son Orestes avenges his father's death by killing the murderous couple, the Fates drive him to Athens for trial. Apollo defends him, and the goddess Athena votes for acquittal. In the process Orestes comes to the realization that the Fates' relentless demand for blood revenge is superseded by a more rational justice, a rule of laws that seeks to harmonize conflicting interests. The rule of reason overcomes blind fate; it is a "court set up in perpetuity" in the heavens.[5]

Sophocles' *Antigone* tells a similar story. When Antigone's brother is slain fighting for his throne at Thebes, she defies King Croesus's edict to let the body rot, and in obedience to a higher law buries her dead. Threatening her with execution, Croesus demands a confession: did she choose flagrantly to disobey?

> Naturally! Since Zeus never promulgated
> Such a law. Nor will you find
> That Justice publishes such laws to man below.
> I never thought your edicts had such force
> They nullified the laws of heaven, which,
> Unwritten, not proclaimed, can boast
> A currency that everlastingly is valid;
> An origin beyond the birth of man.
> And I, whom no man's frown can frighten,
> Am far from risking Heaven's favor by flouting these.[6]

Considering the central role of the poets in Greek education, they undoubtedly exerted a profound influence on the Greek philosophers. Some of the Pre-Socratics openly criticize them for not going far enough. Xenophanes, for example,[7] sees the incongruity of a moral

---

5. See Richard Kuhns, *The House, the City and the Judge: The Growth of Moral Awareness in the Oresteia* (Bobbs-Merrill, 1962).

6. *Antigone*, Second Episode, from *The Oedipus Plays of Sophocles*, trans. Paul Roche (Mentor, 1958), p. 179.

7. For source materials from the Pre-Socratics I am indebted to J. M. Robinson's *An Introduction to Early Greek Philosophy* (Houghton Mifflin, 1968); Philip Wheelwright, ed., *The PreSocratics* (Odyssey, 1966); and Milton S. Nahm, ed., *Selections from Early Greek Philosophy*, 3rd ed. (Appleton-Century-Crofts, 1947).

order in which an impersonal fate produces heroic virtues. He complains that honor, strength, and athletic prowess are irrationally exalted, when in reality they are inferior to wisdom and of far less value to a city. He refers to the vices Homer and Hesiod ascribe to their anthropomorphic gods as vices that in humans are shameful and blameworthy. Instead he declares that Nature and God are one, the all-embracing being, unchanging and all-knowing, and that virtue means wisdom, prudence, and justice rather than the heroic virtues of honor and strength. Heraclitus too is critical of the earlier tradition. He rebukes Homer for wishing that strife might perish from among gods and humans, and chides Hesiod for not seeing what underlies the conflicting forces of nature. For the balance of power between opposing natural forces is a kind of cosmic justice, not a blind fate or the arbitrary doings of gods, and human laws are nourished by one divine law that outlasts them all. Wisdom and justice are therefore the virtues we should desire.

But while the poets are criticized by some, they nonetheless provide the Pre-Socratics with an important starting point. Thales' idea that water is the basic element of which all else is composed seems to echo the Homeric myth that Oceanus was the source of all the gods and everything else.[8] Empedocles talks of love and strife as two forces at work in nature, recalling the two kinds of strife, Love and Hate, in Hesiod's *Theogony*.[9] But more to our point is the comment by Anaximander, that there is a natural equilibrium in which things come into being and pass away

> according to what must be; for they make reparation to one another for their injustice according to the ordinance of time.[10]

Here he plainly breaks with the older view of a capricious nature by enlarging the rule of law he saw in the city-state into the kind of cosmic justice hinted at by the poet Hesiod. The just balance of opposing forces is not only for human societies; it is also a fact in the natural order around us. Opposing properties like dark and light, hot and cold,

---

8. Jaeger, *Theology of the Early Greek Philosophers*, pp. 10, 20.

9. Jaeger, *Theology of the Early Greek Philosophers*, pp. 138-39 and 235-36, nn. 39, 40, and 41.

10. J. M. Robinson, *An Introduction to Early Greek Philosophy*, p. 34. See C. H. Kahn, "Anaximander's Fragment: The Universe Governed by Law," in A. P. D. Mourelatos, *The Pre-Socratics* (Anchor Books, 1974), pp. 99-117.

wet and dry, male and female are all grounded in the same unbounded existence, for neither property is more basic than its opposite and every pair maintains an equilibrium within the whole.

Pythagoras likewise talks of the harmony of opposites in nature and in society, but in the human soul as well. At the individual level, the soul must be purified of irrational impulses by achieving inner harmony and peace. At the societal level, the community must live in harmony within itself, a just life consisting of each member getting his due in proportion to what he has done. Justice is part of a cosmos ordered according to mathematical proportion.

This brings us back to Heraclitus, for he too sees a harmony of opposites grounded in natural law, and calls it *Logos*. Some interpreters take this *Logos* in a descriptive sense only, as a general account of natural processes. Others take it to be a normative law akin to a moral requirement.[11] The Greek term itself has many uses: a statement or account, thought or reason, proportion or measure. Heraclitus's *Logos* is indeed something to be listened to, a message that contrasts with other cosmologies like that of Homer; but it is also something that regulates life, something with an existence independent of our accounts. At times, Heraclitus seems to identify *Logos* with the divine. It is universal reason — the universal law whose justice resolves conflict, introduces stability in a world of constant change, and makes life intelligible. The rationality of the human soul is its most evident manifestation, but the cosmos in its entirety reveals this one divine law to which everything is subject.

. . . all things come to pass in accordance with this Logos.

The universe, which is the same for all, has not been made by any god or man, but it always has been, is, and will be — an ever-living fire, kindling itself by regular measures and going out by regular measures.

Opposition brings concord. Out of discord comes the fairest harmony.

11. See the excellent discussions of Heraclitus's *Logos* by W. K. C. Guthrie, *A History of Greek Philosophy* (Cambridge Univ. Press, 1962), vol. 1, pp. 419-34; and Jonathan Barnes, *The Pre-Socratic Philosophers* (Routledge and Kegan Paul, 1979), vol. 1, ch. 7.

It is by disease that health is pleasant, by evil that good is pleasant, by hunger satiety, by weariness rest.

Men would not have known the name of justice if these things had not occurred.

Justice will overtake fabricators of lies and false witnesses.

Fire in its advance will catch all things by surprise and judge them.

Men should speak with rational awareness and thereby hold strongly to that which is shared in common — as a city holds on to its law, and even more strongly. For all human laws are nourished by one divine law, which prevails as far as it wishes, suffices for all things, and yet is something more than they.[12]

A kind of cosmic justice, a moral ecology, is thus grounded in the reality of the Logos.

A further example of this among the Pre-Socratics is Anaxagoras, who ascribes the natural order to Mind *(Nous)*. Cicero called him "the first human thinker to hold that the orderly disposition of the universe is designed and perfected by the rational power of an infinite mind."[13] This may be an overstatement, for what *Nous* does is just twofold. It initiates motion in a previously motionless conglomeration of material elements. This motion then produces order and animates all living things, causing their activity. Plato has Socrates express disappointment that Anaxagoras failed to ascribe purpose to *Nous,* or any notion of ordering things towards a good end.[14] Anaxagoras does, however, set mind above matter. Matter alone, he implies, fails to explain either the natural order with its functioning of living things or the good we must seek. When asked why anyone should wish to have been born rather than not, he reportedly said it would be for the privilege of contemplating the world-order as a whole; for happiness consists not in the heroic qualities of beauty, power, or wealth, but in "a life without offence to others and conforming to justice or participating in some form of divine con-

12. Excerpts 2, 29, 98-100, 71, 72, and 81 in Wheelwright, *The Pre-Socratics,* pp. 69-79.

13. *De Natura Deorum,* I.11.

14. *Phaedo,* 97b.

templation."[15] That sort of life is part of the natural order *Nous* secures.

Not all Pre-Socratics agreed. In Democritus's mechanistic account of the universe there is no room for cosmic justice or anything approaching it. No cosmic *Nous*, no *Logos* is involved, but only matter, motion, and sheer chance. Instead of trying to replace *Moira* (fate) with *Dike* (justice), Democritus makes fate sheer causal necessity, not just purposeless but mindless, lifeless, and dead. He still moralizes about preventing injustice and obeying the laws, for men are made happy, ultimately, not by fame or fortune but by a balanced life governed by moderation and thoughtfulness rather than passion. Moderation increases pleasure, and to choose wisely is to weigh the pleasurableness of consequences. But this is a hedonistic ethic of expediency grounded in a self-interested assessment of human experience, rather than a larger or more ultimate cosmic order. Likewise, the science of Democritus extends to nature the moral indifference of the Greek fates, reducing the human being to a kind of misfit, a stranded traveler struggling to survive in a bleak, value-neutral world.

While the Sophists came close to Democritus in this regard, they doubted the possibility of knowing the ultimate nature of things at all. The mutually incompatible views of their predecessors made them sceptical of all cosmological inquiry. All I know is what appears to me, declared Protagoras:

> Man is the measure of all things; of those things that are, that they are; of those things that are not, that they are not. . . . As for the gods, I have no way of knowing either that they exist or that they do not exist; nor, if they exist, of what form they are.[16]

So the Sophists turned to rhetoric, that art of persuasion which has the power to make things appear different.

> When persuasion joins with speech it can affect the soul in any way it wishes. . . . The power of speech over the disposition of the soul is comparable to the effect of drugs on the disposition of the body. . . . words can produce grief, pleasure, or fear.[17]

15. Aristotle, *Eudemian Ethics*, 1215B-1216A, cited by Robinson, pp. 191-92.
16. Quoted in Wheelwright, *The Pre-Socratics*, pp. 239-40.
17. *Gorgias*, quoted in Wheelwright, *The Pre-Socratics*, p. 250.

Not surprisingly, Thrasymachus is reported to have said that justice is simply the advantage of the stronger, making it relative to whoever wields the power. No cosmology, no knowledge of divine beings, and no cosmic justice. The dissolution of that vision of reality is complete.

It fell to Socrates to recall Athens to the quest for knowledge, rather than settling for appearances and convention. He thereby enabled Plato to readdress the moral condition of the human soul, and in doing so to bring into focus the idea of a moral universe and its God.

CHAPTER TWO

Plato and the Improvement
of the Soul

ON TRIAL FOR CORRUPTING the youth of Athens, Socrates responded:

> I do nothing but go about persuading you all, old and young alike,
> not to take thought for your persons or your properties, but first and
> chiefly to care about the greatest improvement of the soul. . . . I tell
> you that virtue is not given by money, but that from virtue comes
> money and every other good of man, public as well as private. This
> is my teaching, and if this is the doctrine that corrupts the youth, I
> am a mischievous person.
> . . . I sought to persuade every man among you that he must look
> to himself and seek virtue and wisdom before he looks to his private
> interests, and look to the state before he looks to the [self-]interests
> of the state.[1]

Even the threat of execution did not deter him:

> The difficulty, my friends, is not to avoid death, but to avoid un-
> righteousness.
> And will life be worth living, if that higher part of man be
> destroyed, which is improved by justice and depraved by injustice?[2]

---

1. Plato, *Apology,* 30, 36. All references to Plato are to the Jowett translation
(Random House, 1937).
2. *Apology,* 39; *Crito,* 47.

In presenting this picture of Socrates, Plato discloses the persistent and central concern of his own philosophical work.[3] Many of his dialogues are about the virtues, especially those like justice, wisdom, and prudence. His political writings *(Republic, Statesman, Laws)* likewise address the improvement of the soul; their attention to metaphysics arises only in this context. Commenting later on the guardians he had proposed in his *Republic,* he wrote that they were "to live together in the continual practice of virtue, which was to be their sole pursuit."[4] The art of politics has to do with the soul: what gymnastics and medicine are to the body, legislation and the administration of justice are to the soul.[5]

This concern for the soul even led Plato to criticize Pericles, the popular and gifted Athenian statesman who, Plato said, became a great orator by adding to his rhetorical gifts an attention to reason he had learned from Anaxagoras.[6] In initiating a democratic constitution at home, Pericles had built on Homeric concepts of virtue and justice, but in relationships with other city-states he simply made effective use of political and military power without concern for justice. His rhetoric embraced these conflicting ideals without recognizing that political expediency undermines equal justice for all. Even at home, the policy of remunerating citizens made them idle and encouraged them to love money; and in the end Pericles himself was convicted of theft. Plato argues against this view of justice, as doing good to your friends and evil to your enemies, that it teaches people to be unjust.[7] Pericles should not have given people money, office, or power unless they themselves were gentle and good, and his rhetoric should have aimed to make citizens as good as possible, "to implant justice in their souls and take away injustice, to implant temperance and take away intemperance, to implant virtue and take away every vice."[8]

---

3. See his autobiographical statement in Epistle 7. Of particular help in the light of this concern is Robert E. Cushman, *Therapeia: Plato's Conception of Philosophy* (Univ. of North Carolina Press, 1958).

4. *Timaeus,* 18.

5. *Gorgias,* 464.

6. *Phaedrus,* 270.

7. *Gorgias,* 515-16, 519; *Republic,* 335. See also Alasdair MacIntyre, *Whose Justice? Which Rationality?* (Univ. of Notre Dame Press, 1988), chs. 3 and 4.

8. *Gorgias,* 504, 513-14.

The reason for such attention to the soul is plain. More clearly than at earlier stages in Greek thought, Plato takes the soul to exist prior to the body and to enliven and move it, so that all good and evil originate there. Being immortal, moreover, the soul will have to give an account of itself, "which is an inspiring hope to the good, but very terrible to the bad."[9] This sort of claim raises questions that Plato addresses in a variety of ways, but his central thesis remains the same throughout: the most important task in this life is the improvement of the soul.

This thesis led Plato to criticize poets as well as politicians, Homer as well as Pericles. Since Homer had no firsthand experience as a legislator, statesman, military adviser, inventor, or public servant, he can only copy others' images of the virtues these roles require. He is at his best an imitator who knows only what appears to others to be good or bad.[10] The same criticism is leveled at the rhapsodist, the dramatic interpreter of poets. In the *Ion*, Socrates shows that one who claims to know his Homer does not really know about the horse races, medicine, or fishing portrayed in these epics, and so imparts no reliable knowledge by his acting — unless through some kind of divine inspiration. In his *Republic*, therefore, Plato excludes all poetry from the schools, as it misrepresents virtues or glorifies vices; in this even Homer and his interpreters resemble Sophists.[11]

It was the Sophists who most personified what Plato was against: rhetoric as a way to win wealth or gain power, rather than to instill virtue. He shows the problems with Thrasymachus's definition of justice as whatever benefits the stronger: it assumes that the strong really know what is in their best interest, and hence that they are wiser than the weak; it invites anarchy if people are vying with each other for power; it leads to ignoring justice and even to defending injustice as the better way of life.[12] These criticisms apply to ethical relativism generally: it opens us to ill-conceived self-interest, it threatens what Thomas Hobbes later called "a war of all against all," and it can make no binding moral distinction between good and evil, just and unjust. But above all Thrasymachus reveals his own unknowing stance on whatever subject he addresses.

9. *Laws*, 959; *Republic*, 608-21; *Charmides*, 156-57; *Laws*, 892.
10. *Republic*, 598-600.
11. *Republic*, 377-98; *Protagoras*, 316.
12. *Republic*, 338-52.

This is Plato's concern about sophistical rhetoric in the *Phaedrus*. The orator need only understand the beliefs of his judges, who judge him on the art of persuasion, not on the truth of the matter. The orator can extol evil as being good, and might well persuade the public to do evil instead of good. He influences their souls, but without knowledge and to what end?

The issue is between opinion and knowledge, between appearances and reality. When Protagoras expresses the opinion that "man is the measure of all things," he affirms everybody's opinion, including the opinion that his own opinion is false. So even Protagoras must admit that at least one opinion is wiser than another, and more expedient; but this makes the wiser into the measure of things, not "man" in general, and not everyone equally. Plainly, then, not all opinions are of equal worth.[13]

The relativist is misled into thinking that because the world is continually changing, what once was wise may no longer be so. Everything is in process of becoming; unchanging being is abolished. But because appearances change, it does not follow that the underlying *reality* changes too. This is the point of Plato's famous cave analogy. The Sophist relativist is like a prisoner who, suffering from amnesia and confined to a world of flitting shadows, supposes these appearances to be all the reality there is. If he would think, if he could look behind himself, if he could escape the cave, he would know very differently. This is why the Sophist fails: his rhetoric is not informed by knowledge of the truth, but only by common opinions based on appearances that vary from place to place and from one individual to another. But good and evil are not changing expedients for changing circumstances; they are rooted in a changeless reality unperceived by the senses. How then can a Sophist claim to improve the souls of Athenian youth, while holding such dubious opinions?

But in what sort of reality are values rooted? Here Plato's awareness of his predecessors comes into play. He had applauded Pericles' dependence on Anaxagoras's concept of *Nous* or Mind, and now his own debt to people like Pythagoras becomes apparent. In the *Timaeus,* he states that when everything was in disorder, God set things in order and constructed the cosmos by giving to all things proportion, measure, and harmony. He is echoing Pythagoras's claim that nature has math-

13. *Theaetetus,* 169-72, 177-79.

ematical proportion, limits *(peras)* that give order to otherwise un-limited material elements *(apeiron)*. This cosmic harmony extends to the law-governed city where justice means harmony and proportionate treatment, and to the good life ruled wisely by the soul.

Plato's emphasis on the rational soul producing harmony comes out also in the *Philebus* in regard to the opposition between a life of wisdom and one of wanton pleasure. Neither wisdom nor pleasure alone makes the good life. A measured union of the two is found only in the soul that wisely limits its appetites for pleasure, thus giving rise to inner balance and harmony. As musical harmony depends on math-ematical relationships between notes, so human life must be properly ordered if it is not to end in painful discord and dissolution. "The harmony of the soul is virtue."[14]

The *Republic* develops this picture along parallel lines. There are three elements to the soul: the appetitive, the spirited, and the rational. In both the individual and the state, the problem is to control the unlimited domination by human appetites. But such control is only possible when reason knows the limits and the spirited part has the courage to enforce them. The appetites then gain temperance, the spirit has courage, reason exercises wisdom, and the harmony of the whole makes a just person. In the state this calls for rule by the wise, philos-opher-kings rigorously educated to a disciplined lifestyle aimed at a true understanding and constant pursuit of the good. Plato's theory of forms as unchanging, transcendent ideals becomes relevant here. Reason does not develop opinions about the good and then apply them in governing the appetites. The mind does not create values, but rather it discovers what is objectively and inherently good; what justice really is rather than how it appears to a Thrasymachus or whoever. Values are objectively rooted in reality, and a just government depends on them.

Plato's views on how best to achieve good government changed during his career. The *Republic's* idea of a philosopher-king is modified in the *Statesman* into an all-powerful ruler who can make a community harmonious and unified without imposing invariably fixed and uniform laws. That in turn gives way in the *Laws* to the ideal of a law-governed community in which the people themselves value the good. Moral virtues take precedence over heroic virtues like wealth or beauty. Edu-cation is geared accordingly and should lead the soul "to hate what you

14. *Laws,* 653.

ought to hate and love what you ought to love from the beginning of life to the end." Indeed, a person's whole energies (whether man or woman) throughout life should be devoted to the acquisition of virtue, for Plato concludes that it is not some human but God who ought to be the measure of all things.[15]

Whether Plato is speaking of the individual or the state, he is explicit that knowing the good is essential to the improvement of the soul. His epistemology becomes important. Neither moral ideals like justice nor what he calls the "good" is accessible through sense perception of changing particulars. The unchanging forms are known not by the senses but by "the eye of the mind," a kind of mental insight that results from that painstaking analysis of concepts which he calls "dialectic." It is actually insight into what a soul already knows innately, a kind of "recollection" of forgotten ideas from a previous existence unhampered and undistracted by bodily existence in a physical world. The art of dialectic is acquired only with long and arduous training, but it alone promises the needed knowledge of unchanging ideals.

But several qualifications are in order. First, this is not just a matter of knowledge as against ignorance or opinion, nor just of being able to define or describe a virtue. Discernment between good and evil is required, along with the practiced capacity for making sound judgments that recognize goodness and beauty exemplified in particular cases. Second, it is not a detached, unemotional kind of thinking, but is filled with wonder at and a deep devotion to the good.[16] Plato employs the analogy of a lover absorbed day and night with his beloved, or rather with those ideals that the beloved exemplifies. It is as much *eros,* a passionate desire to have, as it is knowing the good. Third, a distinction repeatedly appears between two loves, a higher and a lower: the lower seeks gratification of earthly desires and drags the soul into a world of restless change; the higher delights in contemplating the eternal, the Form of the Good, Beauty itself, and lifts the soul to changeless and immortal happiness. The *Phaedrus* likens the soul to a charioteer with two winged horses, one wanton and uncontrolled, the other spirited but controllable, soaring towards the sun in all its beauty. As long as the wanton horse is uncontrolled there can be no unified effort, and both horses and charioteers

15. *Laws,* 653, 717, 770.
16. See John Gould, *The Development of Plato's Ethics* (Russell & Russell, 1955), chs. 1-2.

plunge down to earth again and again. But if the driver guides the spirited horse while giving it the lead, then its strength will control the wanton so that they will pull together and soar to the heavens. The analogy is of course to the three elements in the soul — reason, spirit, and appetite — that must be kept in harmony.

> . . . beholding beauty with the eye of the mind, he will be enabled to bring forth, not images of beauty but realities . . . , and bringing forth and nourishing true virtue to become the friend of God and be immortal, if immortal man may. Would that be an ignoble life?[17]

The soul takes on the qualities of whatever it loves, for it is not improved just by knowing, but by desiring and imitating what it supremely loves.

> Wherefore we ought to fly away from earth and heaven as quickly as we can; and to fly away is to become like God, as far as this is possible; and to become like him is to become holy, just, and wise.[18]

The improvement of the soul, then, boils down to the imitation of God, and Plato concludes the *Laws* with that theme: "he who would be dear to God must, as far as is possible, be like him and such as he is."[19] He spells out the qualities this entails: wisdom, temperance, piety, and so forth, qualities he regards as essential in the ideal city-state.

Plato's concept of God emerged only gradually, and what he means remains far from clear. Initially he emphasized simply the forms or ideas of the various virtues, ascribing to them an objective reality independent of any particular exemplifications they might have in our experience. Forms of relationships and of natural classes of things were added, posing questions about what all forms have in common — namely the Form of the Good, the One, and how it relates to the many.[20] The *Timaeus* extends the discussion to cosmology, talking of the Demiurge (a cosmic artificer) and a World Soul (reminiscent of Thales' assertion that everything is "besouled"), while the *Statesman* and the *Laws* talk explicitly of God.

---

17. *Symposium*, 211-12. See *Phaedo*, 78-81; *Phaedrus*, 246-57.

18. *Theaetetus*, 176.

19. *Laws*, 716. See Cuthbert G. Rutenbar, *The Doctrine of the Imitation of God in Plato* (King's Crown, 1946).

20. Particularly in the *Republic* and *Parmenides*.

For all the complexity this presents, several things emerge. First, this entire metaphysical discussion is an attempt to ground values objectively in an unchanging and transcendent reality. Second, Plato's theory of forms introduced a theory of universals with unchanging natures that dominated medieval philosophy and continues to this day. Third, Plato developed the earliest arguments for the existence of God, both teleological and moral arguments. Fourth, Plato's ideas about God anticipated Judeo-Christian ideas and influenced the development of Christian theology.

The Form of the Good is presented in the *Republic* as the transcendent source of all reality, all intelligible order and goodness. This Form, however, though itself the most real being and of supreme value, is not an active, efficient cause of anything. Yet the *Theaetetus,* as we just noted, speaks of God as good, and urges that we imitate him. The Demiurge of the *Timaeus,* who brought cosmic order out of chaos, is also described as good because he desired all things to be good and fashioned them by imitating the eternal forms. As World Soul, he pervades all things, for there can be no intelligence without soul, and the *Philebus* and *Sophist* explicitly link the ordering Mind *(Nous)* to soul.[21] The *Statesman* meantime likens God to a statesman shepherding his people,[22] but it is in the *Laws* that Plato offers his last and most detailed account.[23] God is a self-moving World Soul who orders and inhabits the universe, knows all things, cares about humans and their affairs, rewards good and evil, and has superhuman powers. As ruler of the universe he does everything with a view to the excellence of the whole, each part fulfilling its appropriate role in the overall harmony and balance.

Notably, God is never a world-designer in these accounts, but only an artisan who imitates the forms. He is never a creator bringing

---

21. *Timaeus,* 29-31; *Philebus,* 30; *Sophist,* 249. Etienne Gilson points out that, for the Greeks, "gods" are powers, alive, and include physical things like Oceanus, Earth, and Sky. Plato also uses the term for other powers than the Demiurge, including human souls. See *God and Philosophy* (Yale Univ. Press, 1941), ch. 1; also R. Hackforth, "Plato's Theism," in R. E. Allen, ed., *Studies in Plato's Metaphysics* (Humanities, 1965). F. M. Cornford in *Plato's Cosmology* (Harcourt, Brace, 1937) argues that the World Soul is merely symbolic of the order of the cosmos.

22. *Statesman,* 269-75.

23. *Laws,* 894-903.

the cosmos into existence out of nothing, but only its orderer, forming things from uncreated matter. He is conceived to be the soul of the universe, its inner guide and life source, rather than the active yet transcendent and self-sufficient deity of the Judeo-Christian tradition. But he is powerful, purposeful, intelligent, and good in an outgoing way: everything he makes is directed towards the overall goodness of the universe. Individual virtue and the just city-state are parts of this cosmic harmony, and because they imitate God's goodness they are microcosms of the whole.

The parallel between the cosmos and the human soul is striking. In the *Republic,* the *Phaedrus,* and elsewhere, it is the soul that rules the body, and its intelligent element that rules the spirited and appetitive parts, imitating the forms and bringing order out of chaos for the good of the whole. The chief purpose of the *Timaeus* seems to be to link morality to the organization of the cosmos. Values are grounded in reality, in the forms, in the nature of soul, in cosmic harmony, in the idea of the good, in God.

> The ruler of the universe has ordered all things with a view to the excellence and preservation of the whole, and each part, as far as may be, has an action and passion appropriate to it. Over these, down to the last fraction of them, ministers [individual souls] have been appointed to preside, . . . one of these portions of the universe is thine own, unhappy man, which, however little, contributes to the whole, and in order that the life of the whole may be blessed; and that you are created for the sake of the whole, and not the whole for the sake of you.[24]

Yet disharmony constantly occurs in the cosmos, evil as well as good. Plato blames the soul's appetitive element for an individual's unruly conduct, which must be kept in check by spirited passion aroused by reason. He advises us to think about and learn from "the harmonies and revolutions of the universe" in order to attain the good of the soul.[25] Analogously in the world at large, nature's processes have a tendency not only towards harmonious unity but also towards destruction, unless they are kept in order and harnessed to good ends. When God lets go, the world revolves in a reverse direction due to the

24. *Laws,* 903.
25. *Timaeus,* 90; see also 69-70.

weight of matter and its original chaotic nature.[26] The *Laws* suggests that another world soul, the Dyad, a companion of folly rather than wisdom, at times moves things wildly and irregularly.[27]

Evil, then, has natural causes that do not serve the good. This is the case both in the cosmos at large and in human experience. It gives increased importance to the improvement of the soul, but it also opens the door to the dualistic interpretations, later developed by the Gnostics, that Aristotle strove to avoid. Even so, Plato's idealism about good grounded in cosmic reality and the goodness of God would inevitably attract the interest and admiration of some early Christians. We shall return to this matter in Chapter 4, but we should first take a look at Aristotle's development of another Platonic idea rooted in the Pre-Socratics — that of a natural teleology.

26. *Statesman*, 269-75.
27. *Laws*, 896-97.

CHAPTER THREE

Aristotle and Nature's Teleology

IN THEIR THINKING about the cosmos, the early Greek philosophers struggled to distinguish between appearances and reality. Plato and Aristotle extended this concern into the ethical domain where what appears to some to be the good may not in reality be so. Pleasure, wealth, power, or success may be sought after because to their devotees they appear to be the highest end, but in reality they are not. This confusion between appearance and reality in ethics underlies the contest between two dominant images of human life that Alasdair MacIntyre finds in post-Homeric reflection, a life aiming at virtue or excellence *(arete)* and a life aiming at success or power.[1] The former image is found in Plato and Aristotle, the latter in Aristotle's one-time student, Alexander the Great. Neither power nor success, nor pleasure, nor wealth is in reality the highest good, even though to some people they appear so.

Of course, Plato and Aristotle had their differences. Plato's vision of one ideal society was essentially utopian. Aristotle, a non-utopian, saw a variety of feasible political arrangements. But both were concerned for the improvement of the soul and developed an ethic of virtue grounded in the ordered nature of reality as a whole. Not surprisingly, both were later adopted by Christian thinkers and their views "Christianized."

Yet their differences are marked. Plato was much more the moral-

---

1. Alasdair MacIntyre, *Whose Justice? Which Rationality?* (Univ. of Notre Dame Press, 1988), p. 88.

ist, the would-be reformer, the political idealist whose entire philosophy, as we have seen, was driven by ethical concerns. Aristotle, on the other hand, seems more the objective scientist detached from immediate historical concerns. He was not continually wrestling with the Sophists and their relativism, and hence preoccupied with the search for transcendent norms; his emphasis is rather on the ordered unity in the nature of things we actually experience.[2] In fact, Whitney Oates complains that Aristotle develops his theory of being in isolation from values and his theory of values in isolation from God.[3] Whether this is the case or not, Aristotle's ethic is still grounded in his metaphysic, and there are at least hints of the relation between human virtue and the divine. Being is not value-neutral. The difference, rather, is that in contrast to the pervasive priority of ethics in Plato's thinking and the independence of the forms from all temporal particulars, Aristotle holds values to be "in a secondary and dependent status in relation to nature."[4] He declares forms to be immanent in particulars, so that the world of particulars is laden with value-potential through and through. Morality then is grounded in nature's teleology, and the nature of this teleology is the key to his ethic and to his differences from Plato.

Aristotle's relation to Plato has been the subject of extended debate. Werner Jaeger saw Aristotle as primarily a critic of his former mentor's work. Recent scholarship takes a more positive stance; MacIntyre, for example, claims that Aristotle tends to complete lines of inquiry that Plato had begun.[5] This surely is the case with regard to teleology in nature. While Aristotle was initially sold on Plato's theory of forms, he later found it an inadequate explanation of nature's processes, and he had problems with Plato's Form of the Good in ethics. His best-known criticisms of the doctrine of forms appear in *Metaphysics*, I, and deal largely with their relation to the world of particulars. Similarily in *Physics*, II.2, he complains that mathematical objects

2. This contrast is suggested by Marjorie Greene in *A Portrait of Aristotle* (Univ. of Chicago Press, 1963), pp. 51-52.

3. Whitney J. Oates, *Aristotle and the Problem of Value* (Princeton Univ. Press, 1963), pp. ix, 4.

4. Oates, *Aristotle and the Problem of Value*, p. 320.

5. See Werner Jaeger, *Aristotle* (Oxford Univ. Press, 1934); G. E. L. Owen, "The Platonism of Aristotle," *Proceedings of the Aristotelian Society* 50 (1965); MacIntyre, *Whose Justice?* ch. 6; W. K. C. Guthrie, *A History of Greek Philosophy*, vol. 6: *Aristotle: An Encounter* (Cambridge Univ. Press, 1981).

(forms) are artificially separated from physical objects despite the patent fact that they are essential to the very nature and existence of anything physical. By boiling everything down to two causes, form and matter, Plato makes form (and the One) the cause of all that is good and matter (the dyad) the cause of evil.[6] But can the One, the Form of the Good, effectively meet that demand?

Aristotle's ethical writings press this line of thought further. First, "good" is used of things in various categories — substances, qualities, and relations — yet substance is so basic to the others that "good" has a different sense there than elsewhere. No one meaning of "good" is possible throughout, and no one science of the good.[7] Second, in all these senses Plato thinks the good is ultimately found in the mind of God, but as such it only functions as an ideal pattern with no effective power over particulars.[8] Nor is there anything in the nature of a particular to incline it to the good, but only matter, which for Plato is resistant to form. If Plato's Form of the Good, like the forms themselves, is a powerless if not meaningless ideal, then we need a different way of thinking about these things.

Aristotle's dissatisfaction with all his predecessors extends to what they say about the natural causes of order, beauty, and good. Anaxagoras's cosmic Mind certainly went beyond others' attention to simply material causes, and Empedocles' appeal to love and strife added a *source* of order, beauty, and good. But they are too unscientific for Aristotle: Anaxagoras's Mind is a *deus ex machina,* an ad hoc hypothesis pulled in when all else fails; Empedocles is too unsystematic. Plato really went no further than they did; his two causes, form and matter, have to account for good and evil just like Anaxagoras's Mind and matter or Empedocles' love and strife.[9] The problem Aristotle sees is not just one of explaining change, but of explaining change that by its very nature produces order, beauty, and good.

If his predecessors were too unscientific, then an improved method becomes important. How can we discover the essential causes of natural processes, rather than simply spotting one or two necessary factors? The inductive method he describes in the *Posterior Analytics* (distinct from

6. *Metaphysics,* I.6.
7. *Nicomachean Ethics,* 1096a.
8. *Eudemian Ethics,* 1217b.30-31.
9. *Metaphysics,* I.3, 4, 6; XII.10.

the modern inductive methods introduced by Francis Bacon and John Stuart Mill) amasses and classifies sensory input about a class of things until it becomes one unified experience in which a general course of events is clear. The general rule reveals the universal potential in that class of things, its inner essence or form. (Our term "essence" is simply a translation of his *ti estin,* "what it is.") Things change as they do, then, not randomly but by virtue of what in fact they are. That is why change tends to follow some form.

> Our first presupposition must be that in nature nothing acts on, or is acted on, by any other thing at random, nor can anything come from anything else, unless we mean that it does so in virtue of a concomitant attribute. . . . Nor again do things pass into the first chance thing.[10]

To say something happens "by chance" does not mean it is un-caused but only that it is contrary to the general rule. It is an incidental happening, caused by extraneous factors rather than the essence of a thing, and it can result in either good or evil. I am out walking for exercise when I "happen" to meet someone I needed to talk with. It was a "chance" meeting, and it was "good" that we ran into each other. Aristotle confines his use of "chance" to human activities; more broadly he speaks of "spontaneity" as an incidental cause in animals and inanimate things as well as in humans, in contrast to the essential nature of a process.[11] His point is that nothing is random or uncaused: nature follows general patterns to predictable ends. But, in addition to material causes and forms with their natural ends, efficient causes have also to be reckoned with. That is where chance and spontaneity come in.

This is important for Aristotle's handling of the mistakes and failures in nature that produce disorder and evil.[12] Such failures occur not because nature is an inherently chaotic array of random forces, or because matter is resistant to order. They occur, rather, when in the complexity of things the natural process is impeded by incidental outside causes. In human actions, each step is followed by another for the

10. *Physics,* 188a.32-35; 188b.3.

11. *Physics,* II.4, 5. See also W. Wieland, "The Problem of Teleology," *Articles on Aristotle: 1, Science,* ed. Jonathan Barnes et al. (Duckworth, 1975), p. 127.

12. *Physics,* II.8; *Categories,* xi.

sake of an end, unless something accidentally interferes. Natural processes likewise follow their general course to predictable ends, provided nothing interferes. Interference sometimes occurs, of course, and deformities ensue, but as a general rule normal natural processes are orderly and the results are good.

At times Aristotle draws an analogy between nature and human action in ascribing purpose to nature.

> It is absurd to suppose that purpose is not present because we do not observe the agent deliberating. Art does not deliberate. If the ship-building art were in the wood, it would produce the same result *by nature*. If, therefore, purpose is present in art, it is present also in nature. The best illustration is a doctor doctoring himself: nature is like that. It is plain then that nature is a cause, a cause that operates for a purpose.[13]

The point seems to be that purposes need not be conscious. The doctor and the artist do not deliberate over ends: the doctor asks *how* to heal, not whether; the shipbuilder thinks about *how* to build a ship, not whether. It is their nature as doctor and shipbuilder to seek to heal and to produce ships. Nature's ends, while not always conscious, are not matters of chance; they are potencies inherent in the essential nature of things.

A "potency" or "potential" is a dynamic (Gk. *dunamis*) capacity for a certain kind of change, or for resisting another kind of change (as in a hard rock that resists being broken). Some potencies are learned (like crafts), some come by practice (like playing the flute), but some are innate, natural endowments. Without these capacities, there would be no craftsmen, no music, no heat or cold, no sweet or sour, for they all depend on our sensory powers; one could not see or hear without those powers. In fact, without capacity there is only incapacity, and without possibility there would only be impossibility: nothing could happen, nothing could change, nothing could become what in fact it generally is. For all change is the actualizing of some potential, whatever the kind of change may be.[14] Potential lies in the actual possession of some quality: the actual quality of an acorn makes it potentially an oak, the actual quality of an infant makes it potentially an adult, the actual quality of marble makes it potentially a sculpture. This is where form

13. *Physics*, 199b.26-33.
14. *Metaphysics*, V.12; IX; *Physics*, III.1.

comes into the picture, for form is the essence of things. A human being is potentially a rational animal, and rationality is the essence or form of the species. The potential for a full, rational life is then inherent within us, and its fulfillment is our natural end. This is the natural order of things, and it is good.

Aristotle finds four kinds of cause at work in both nature and art, not only matter and necessary efficient causes as the Pre-Socratics suggest, nor just form and matter as in Plato. The idea of final cause is added as the end *(telos)* to which a process generally leads and for whose sake it goes on at all. Things may not consciously desire their ends, as humans often do; but natural ends are the good that nature generally achieves, the good therefore that we should desire. The distinction between moral appearance and moral reality now has basis: the good is not just what appears desirable, but it is grounded in nature, in what a thing really is, its essence.

Here then is a teleology that pervades everything. Nothing can be adequately explained without it, and nothing exists independently of it. "God and nature," says Aristotle, "create nothing that has not its use." "Nature never makes anything without a purpose."[15] But this is an immanent teleology inherent in the very nature of things, not a transcendent purpose directed by an outside power. The potency is nature's own, and so therefore are the ends.

Yet nature functions as a coordinated whole, and its processes go on endlessly as if for some common *telos*. Aristotle therefore argues repeatedly for the existence of one, eternal Unmoved Mover who somehow moves the heavenly spheres (and indirectly everything else) to emulate his own perfection. To be unmoved, unchanging, the Unmoved Mover can have no unfulfilled potential; he is pure actuality, pure form without matter; nor can he be affected by anything else, nor even act on other things as an efficient cause, nor even think about them, for all of this would actualize something in him, implying potential. The Unmoved Mover is therefore not an efficient cause of nature and its processes, but only its final cause. He did not, does not, and cannot create or change anything. But he *is*, and he is pure being with no becoming, and that is completely good.

To be pure actuality — the one self-sufficient, self-maintaining, and eternal being — is the highest conceivable good. His sole activity

15. *On the Heavens*, 271a.33; *On the Soul*, 432b.21.

is thinking on his own thinking, that is, contemplation. This kind of goodness, this complete actualization, is the unifying end of all natural desires. Those who deny a sole Prime Mover and opt instead for an infinite series of causes "eliminate the Good without knowing it."[16] But, says Aristotle,

> If God is always in that good state in which we sometimes are, this compels our wonder: and if in a better this compels it yet more. And God *is* in a better state. And life belongs to God; for the actuality of thought is life, and God is that actuality; and God's self-dependent actuality is life most good and eternal. We say therefore that God is a living being, eternal, most good, so that life and duration continuous and eternal belong to God; for this *is* God.[17]

These words remind us of Plato's Form of the Good; indeed, Neoplatonism later identified Plato's Good with Aristotle's Unmoved Mover. The ascription of "life" to God also reminds us of Plato's World Soul, and pure "thought" echoes Plato's *Nous* or Mind. Soul, or life, for Aristotle, is both the cause of a living body and its efficient cause, its form or essence and its final cause;[18] and nature is enlivened by God, since its final cause is the Unmoved Mover. Moreover, since for Aristotle thinking is the activity of active intellect, some interpreters take the Unmoved Mover to be a cosmic Mind, immanent in nature as a whole. But Aristotle is not explicit at this point. He discusses briefly whether the nature of the universe contains the highest good as something separate and by itself or as the order of the parts, and responds "probably both."[19] The Unmoved Mover is at least *qualitatively* other than nature, an immaterial intelligence rather than an embodied soul. But being neither conscious of what goes on in the natural world, nor an efficient cause, it cannot be regarded as either creator or providential ruler in any theistic sense, nor as a personal moral agent.[20]

Aristotle's teleological understanding of nature includes the human person. And, since the good is what all things aim at, ethics therefore has to do with the human *telos* and its actualization. What then is the essential

16. *Metaphysics,* 994b.12; see also XII.6-7; *Physics,* VIII.
17. *Metaphysics,* 1072b.23-29.
18. *On the Soul,* II.4.
19. *Metaphysics,* XII.10.
20. See Oates, *Aristotle and the Problem of Value,* pp. 248-53.

nature of a human being, and what is the potential to be actualized? The *Nicomachean Ethics* briefly summarizes a philosophical psychology already worked out in *On the Soul.* The soul is not only the efficient cause of bodily functions, it is the essence of the person, having the natural potencies that characterize humans. In all living species a vegetative soul has powers of nutrition and growth; these are no different in humans than in other living things. In all animals, an appetitive soul has powers of sensation and movement, but in humans these powers are subject to rational guidance. The human soul is distinguished by its power to think, which Aristotle distinguishes from irrational elements such as "rational soul" or mind *(Nous).* The power to think is just that, a potentiality that before it is actualized is not any real thing; it has no nature of its own other than the capacity to think.[21] But it naturally develops from potential (or passive) intellect to actual (or active) intellect. It can think both practically and speculatively, and so a further distinction is introduced between practical and speculative reason.

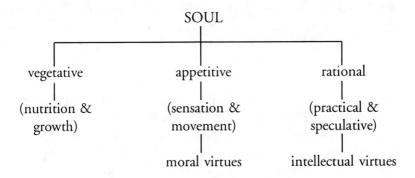

The good, the human *telos,* is the full development of all this potential. This is our highest good. It is *eudaimonia,* usually translated "happiness" but actually closer to "well-being," although "well" simply reiterates "good." Aristotle elaborates: the human good is the activity of soul (i.e., an actualized life) in accordance with virtue *(arete).* Virtue means excellence, fulfilled potential of every sort, a human flourishing in full possession and use of our natural powers.[22] Moral virtues are

21. *On the Soul,* 429a.21-25. See also *Nicomachean Ethics,* I.13.

22. *Nicomachean Ethics,* I.4. John Cooper translates *eudaimonia* as "human flourishing," in *Reason and the Human Good in Aristotle* (Harvard Univ. Press, 1975), ch. 1.

the excellence of the appetitive life, intellectual virtues of the life of the mind.

Such human flourishing is lacking in those who live for pleasure, wealth, or honor, for other animals have such appetites too; only humans have the power to think and so to guide those appetites. The human *telos* does not exclude pleasure or other such satisfactions; on the contrary, it requires enough external goods to make doing good possible,[23] and achieving the good brings its own pleasure. The good, then, is to live a complete life.

> For one swallow does not make a summer, nor does one day; and so too one day or short time does not make a man blessed or happy.[24]

Actualizing such a life is a developmental process. Nature gives the capacity, but to develop it requires right habits, and right habits require right choices repeatedly made and reinforced until they become second nature. Right choices in turn must be determined by practical reason deliberating about what is good and expedient. The various appetites, and pleasure and pain in general, may be felt both too much and too little, and neither is good. But to feel them "at the right times, with reference to the right objects, towards the right people, with the right motive and in the right way," mediates between these extremes and characterizes virtue.[25] So the intellectual virtue of practical wisdom underlies the development of moral virtue in the appetitive life.

But what about people who lack such wisdom? In the case of young children, discipline that shapes behavioral habits helps their development. Aristotle in fact cites three classes of people who are unable to govern themselves wisely and who should therefore be ruled by others, a list that today would elicit protest: young children, women, and others who "by nature" are slaves because they too lack sufficiently active intellects of their own.

More significant is the role he gives the state, and this too stems from his view of human nature: we are not just gregarious individuals but, by virtue of our rational nature, political beings who order our lives and communities by integrating different activities and purposes for the good.

23. *Nicomachean Ethics,* 1099a.31-1099b.8.
24. *Nicomachean Ethics,* 1098a.18-19.
25. *Nicomachean Ethics,* 1106b.15-28.

The state is thus a creation of nature, and the best kind of state exists not just to provide external goods but for the good of the soul — in effect, to make men good. Since practical reason is fallible and can be misguided, the state therefore inculcates right habits by means of just laws.[26]

What of speculative or contemplative reason? Aristotle deals with it rather briefly and not altogether clearly. The highest happiness *(eudaimonia)* is found in contemplative activity that takes thought of things noble and divine. It is highest for a number of reasons: it is the activity of our best power; it is more continuous than intermittent deeds; it is more purely pleasurable, something we love for itself; and it can be enjoyed independently of other activities. But, he adds, such a life is too high for mere humans. Our bodily nature is such that we need health and food if we are to exercise the intellect, and this interrupts thinking. But contemplation is God's sole activity: for him alone is it self-sufficient, and the gods must surely delight in what is most akin to themselves.[27]

For all its brevity, this passage is highly suggestive. Contemplation is indeed the only activity of the Unmoved Mover, thinking on his thinking, although it was certainly not the only activity of the traditional Greek gods. Yet Aristotle speaks of contemplating as God contemplates, and happiness *(eudaimonia,* "well-being") and virtue *(arete,* "excellence") he calls "God-like" things. Moreover, he assigns to the state the care of religion and worship, providing for priests and temples at public expense.[28] What are we to make of all this?

From what we know of Aristotle's own religious outlook,[29] he respected mystical experience and the inner religious life, and spoke piously of the imperishable universe. Seneca credits him with saying we should be nowhere more modest than in matters of religion, and with having feelings of awe in the presence of the divine. To conclude with Seneca that Aristotle thought of the universe as a sacred temple and of reason as the divine within us may be reading too much Stoicism

---

26. *Politics,* I.1-2; VII.1-3. Alasdair MacIntyre (in *Whose Justice?* ch. 6) infers that one cannot be practically rational apart from membership in some particular *polis.*

27. *Nicomachean Ethics,* X.7-8.

28. *Politics,* VII.8-12.

29. I am indebted here to Anton-Herman Chroust, *Aristotle: New Light on His Life and on Some of His Lost Works* (Univ. of Notre Dame Press, 1973), vol. 1, ch. 16, "Aristotle's Religious Consciousness."

back into Aristotle. But it is at least clear that contemplative reason looks beyond the immediacies of this life, beyond the choices of practical reason, beyond even the human soul. As Henry Veatch puts it, the most important end of knowledge is not a knowledge of humankind, because humans are not the most important thing in the universe.[30] The very nature of our being points us beyond ourselves. Aristotle may or may not have connected human contemplation with the Unmoved Mover, but the direction of his thinking points that way: the good is grounded in human nature, but humans are not the measure of all things, for only God is perfectly good. In reality, the human *telos,* our highest end, is God. We shall return to this theme in Chapter 5.

30. *Aristotle: A Contemporary Appreciation* (Indiana Univ. Press, 1974), pp. 125-27.

CHAPTER FOUR

The Divine Logos and the Goodness of Creation

FROM NEW TESTAMENT TIMES onward, Christianity and Greek philosophy came into repeated contact. The apostle Paul, addressing an audience of Stoics and Epicureans in Athens, cited the Stoic philosopher Cleanthes' *Hymn to Zeus* as testimony to a divine Creator, and his language about natural morality in Romans 1 and 2 evokes reflection on Stoic natural law.[1] The letters of both Paul and John reveal that Christians were interacting with current philosophical ideas; and the church fathers of the first three centuries not only cite pagan writers whom they think support their belief in one God, but they also note what in those philosophers and poets deserves acceptance and what does not.

Plato in particular was regarded favorably: not only Plato, to be sure, but the Stoics to some extent also, especially on matters of ethics. But Plato receives the most widespread praise. Justin Martyr, for instance, himself a philosopher-turned-evangelist, applauds both Plato's idea of a transcendent, incorporeal, and unchanging God by whom the cosmos was created and on whom it depends, and the belief that, like God, the soul is a rational being. He does this despite Plato's notion that the soul is inherently immortal and subject to cycles of reincarnation. In similar fashion, Clement of Alexandria praises Plato for seeing that God is One, the creator who gave order to the cosmos, whom we

---

1. Acts 17:16-34.

should contemplate and seek to be like. Origen refers to Plato's belief in the goodness and transcendence of the creator, the goodness of the material world, and the soul's need for purification. Augustine subsequently sums it up with an extended discussion in book VIII of his *City of God:* Plato is justly to be preferred to all the other philosophers because he says God is the cause of the creation, the source of the light of truth, the end in reference to which life is to be regulated by imitation, and because he affirmed the immateriality and immortality of the soul.[2]

To understand why they singled out these features of Plato's thought, we have not only to recognize the obvious parallels to Christian theology — still at a very formative stage in the second and even the third century — but also to see the encroachments of Gnosticism. Early hints of it appear in the New Testament. In his Colossian letter, Paul refers to the asceticism associated with the worship of various "powers" and "spirits of the universe." Elsewhere, to ascetics who forbade marriage, he responds that everything God created is good, and he warns against "the godless chatter and contradictions of what is falsely called knowledge."[3] John argues against those who denied that Christ "came in the flesh" by claiming "we have heard . . . seen with our eyes . . . looked upon and touched with our hands" the living Logos.[4]

Gnosticism was a mixture of Greek and Eastern ideas, sometimes with Jewish or Christian overtones. According to a typical version of it, God is utterly transcendent and unknown, but there emanates from him a hierarchy of spirits and powers that include both angelic beings and human souls. One such power, out of *hybris,* asserted its independence of God, ran amok and formed the material world by some tragic accident. A dualism of spirit and matter resulted, with matter ruled by the powers of darkness and therefore evil. God, in this system, is not the creator of all, and the world is not good. Human beings are trapped in an alien sphere, condemned to ignorance in a darkened world where all we can do is avoid its enticements with ascetic discipline. The only hope of escape lies in discovering esoteric secrets about the unknown

---

2. A. H. Armstrong cites these and other Christian responses to Greek philosophy in *The Cambridge History of Later Greek and Early Medieval Philosophy* (Cambridge Univ. Press, 1967).

3. 1 Tim. 4:3-4, RSV.

4. 1 John 1:1-2, RSV.

God, which will shed the light of truth and dispel the darkness of ignorance from the human mind. This secret knowledge, *gnosis,* Gnostic religion purported to offer its devotees.[5]

The Gnostics' claim that the physical creation is devoid of value threatened Christianity on many fronts. If matter is evil, then an altogether good and transcendent God could not incarnate himself in human flesh; at best Christ only *appeared* to have a body. This "docetic" view of Christ had to be contested. If matter is evil, moreover, then asceticism is required and marriage could not be ordained by God. Nor are the riches of nature's harvest the gifts of God to be enjoyed. The benefits of culture should also be spurned. And if escape lies in securing the secret *gnosis,* then salvation is gained by knowledge, not by faith. This was a very different gospel from what the apostles preached.

Gnosticism denies the basic fact-value relationship envisioned by the Pre-Socratics, and by Plato and Arisotle. Its eternal conflict between good and evil allows no cosmic justice, and its negative view of the material world allows no inner *telos* and denies that creation is ordered for good. Thus, while Gnosticism posed theological problems for the early church, it also discarded what had become the dominant Greek view, that value is rooted in reality.

In the face of Gnosticism, the Stoics and Plato looked good. Stoicism, apparently building on Heraclitus, asserted that the cosmos is governed by a rational law, the divine logos, and that seeds of the logos, *logoi spermatikoi,* enliven and govern every living thing and provide human beings with rational souls. God then is not remote and transcendent, related to this world only via a hierarchy of emanating spirits; he is not far from any of us: "in him we live and move and have our being," Cleanthes had said. God is the ever-living Logos, immanent in everything, a corporeal being of which the human soul is itself a seed, a divine spark. This Stoic pantheism, contrasted with Gnostic dualism, sees God as rational and good, the world too, and the human body. Matter is not evil, running amok, but good.

This appealed to the church father Tertullian, struggling as he was with Gnosticism and its Docetist outcome, for it enabled him to affirm one God as maker of heaven and earth, and hence the goodness of all

5. On ancient Gnosticism, see Kurt Rudolph, *Gnosis,* trans. R. M. Wilson (Harper and Row, 1983); and Gilles Quispel, "Gnosticism," *Encyclopedia of Religion,* ed. Mircea Eliade (Macmillan, 1987), vol. 5, pp. 566-74.

creation. Moreover, if the rational soul too is corporeal, as Stoics held, then corporeal things are not per se evil. Tertullian adopted their "traducian" theory that each individual's soul, being corporeal, is transmitted in sexual reproduction. If sex brings the rational soul to birth, then sex must be of God: it is not evil but good, and so then is marriage. Gnostic dualism, in which matter is evil, Incarnation is denied, and asceticism embraced, is thus overcome with one stroke by the adoption of Stoic beliefs.[6]

This was no doubt an attractive way of responding to Gnosticism, for it grounded values in the Logos-structure of a law-governed reality. But the price was more than other church fathers were willing to pay. They preferred Plato's account of a transcendent God and the immateriality of the soul. Plato's God, the Demiurge, ordered the creation for good ends on the pattern of eternal forms, and the creation is enlivened and governed by an immanent World Soul. The material world, therefore, is not itself evil, but rationally formed and good, and the improvement of the soul is possible by loving contemplation of the eternal forms and of God. Values again are grounded in an ordered reality.

But early Christian writers were not satisfied simply to cull helpful ideas from the Greeks. They puzzled over how these pagans came to know so much. As Justin Martyr asked, "How can the philosophers speculate correctly or speak truly of God, when they have no knowledge of him, since they have never seen or heard him?"[7] The language here is a patent allusion to the words of John's first letter, cited above: how can those who have not seen and heard and touched the incarnate Logos declare the truth about God? Plato himself observed that "the father and maker of all this universe is past finding out, and even if we found him, to tell him to all men would be impossible."[8]

Justin replies that Plato borrowed from Moses, having learned of him while in Egypt, but then disguised the truth for fear of the hemlock.[9] Clement similarily suggests that Plato learned from those "wiser than the Greeks," in this case the Hebrews who honor the immortal God.[10] Augustine considers whether Plato might have met Jeremiah in

---

6. See Tertullian's *Against Marcion* and *Treatise on the Soul*.

7. *Dialogue with Trypho*, iv. His initial response to the question is that God is "to be perceived by the mind alone, as Plato affirms."

8. *Timaeus*, 28. Clement agreed: see his *Exhortation to the Greeks*, vi.59.

9. *Hortatory Address to the Greeks*, xxii-xxviii; *First Apology*, lix-lx.

10. *Exhortation to the Greeks*, vi.60.

Egypt, but he quickly realizes that Plato was there much later than Jeremiah and too early to have read the Septuagint translation of the Old Testament. So the hypothesis that Plato borrowed from Judaism seemed to have little if any basis. How then did he discover the truth?

Another explanation appears in the patristic writings, one which appeals to John's statements about the Logos at the outset of his gospel:

> In the beginning was the Word, and the Word was with God, and the Word was God. He was in the beginning with God; all things were made through him, and without him was not anything made that was made. In him was life, and the life was the light of men . . . the true light that enlightens every man was coming into the world.[11]

Justin Martyr asserts that Plato and others like him, through their "participation of the seminal Divine Word" and "by means of the engrafted seed of the Word which was implanted in them, had a dim glimpse of the truth."[12] Their understanding was certainly incomplete and sometimes they contradict what Christians believe, for they have only seeds of truth and do not know the whole Logos, Jesus Christ. So also Clement: the glimpses of truth in pagan writers point to Christ the Logos, for we are "rational images formed by God's Word."[13] Origen too ascribes the truth that pagans perceive to universal ideas implanted in the souls of all people by the divine Logos.[14] Philosophy in fact was to the Greeks what the Law was for Jews: it prepared them for Christ. So the seeds of truth in the philosophers belong also to Christians, who can reunite them to the whole truth about the Logos from which they were torn. Whereas Gnosticism produced an unreflective acceptance of a secret gnosis, Christianity properly values the truth it finds in the philosophy and culture of the Greeks. All truth is God's truth no matter where it is found. ⟨- disagree

But the church fathers, following the suggestion in John's gospel, see Christ not only as the Logos of all human knowledge but also as

---

11. John 1:1-4, 9, RSV. Cp. Heb. 1:1-3, 10-12. On John's Logos and its Jewish and pre-Christian background, see J. D. G. Dunn, *Christology in the Making* (Westminster, 1980), ch. 7.

12. *First Apology,* xlvi; *Second Apology,* xiii.

13. *Exhortation to the Greeks,* i.6; xii.93.

14. *Contra Celsum,* I.iv.3; *De Principiis,* I.ii.

the Logos of creation by whom all things were made, and who remains immanent in everything. This they are all quick to admit, Tertullian included, as something the Stoics rightly saw, however imperfectly and incompletely. Having their seeds of truth commingled with error, the Stoics did not know the whole Logos. Nonetheless, because the Logos of creation was revealed in the Incarnation, the church fathers affirmed that creation is good, contrary to the Gnostics. The inadequacies they saw in both Stoicism and Platonism led them to doctrines about God and the Logos that have distinguished Christianity from Greek philosophy to this day, claiming a more satisfactory basis for both good and evil than the Greeks at their best achieved.

What then distinguishes the Christian from the Greek Logos? To get at this, we need to look more closely at the Middle Platonism those Christian writers were acquainted with.[15] A varied and eclectic movement, Middle Platonism provided philosophical justification for the pagan Greek and Roman religion that had been undergoing a first-century revival. Plato's God, the One or Good, was of course very remote and transcendent, and Plato himself had problems explaining how things in this world could participate in the eternal forms that served as archetypes for the divine Maker. But Middle Platonists treated the traditional gods as belonging to a hierarchy of intermediary beings, necessary agents in both the divine and the cosmic economy. They retained the Demiurge of Plato's *Timaeus,* equating him with the Mind *(Nous)* in which all the eternal forms resided, and identified this with the Stoic *Logos.* About Plato's World Soul they were less clear, although some of them agreed with Plato that it was the active agent in creation. A kind of divine trinity thus emerged: the One, then the Logos known as *deuteros theos* (second god), and the World Soul.

Others accepted as rational and good only the One and the *Nous,* calling it the Monad. Influenced by the Pythagorean dualism of *peras* (form) and *apeiron* (formlessness), they equated Logos with *peras* and World Soul with *apeiron* and Plato's Dyad, that formless receptacle on which order had to be imposed. Since matter itself is chaotic and therefore the source of evil, only form and reason can save us. In both this and the trinitarian version, ascetic tendencies developed, alongside

15. See John Dillon, *The Middle Platonists* (Cornell Univ. Press, 1977); and Armstrong, ed., *The Cambridge History of Later Greek and Early Medieval Philosophy,* pt. 1.

the primary emphasis on contemplation of unchanging forms and the imitation of God.

A salient Middle Platonist theme that attracted Christians was of course the divine Logos within an eternal trinity.[16] This provides the needed link between a transcendent God and his creation, one that ascribes to God himself the rational ordering of creation. It involved changing the Stoic view that corporeal seeds of the cosmic Logos govern nature into a more Platonic or Pythagorean view of *logoi* as immaterial forms immanent in all finite things; thereby both the world and rational souls participate in eternal archetypes in the divine *Nous* or Logos. Christ is then the Logos both of human knowledge and of creation.

The first-century Alexandrian Jew Philo had puzzled over the gulf between a transcendent God and his creation, introducing a hierarchy of intermediaries of whom the Logos is the highest. God is good, the Monad who first creates the forms within his own mind, and then the sensible world made on their pattern. The Logos is the totality of those forms, the divine wisdom, an overall rational order conceived by God and now operative in creation much like Plato's World Soul.

> For God, being God, pledged in advance that a beautiful copy would never be produced except from a beautiful pattern and that no sense object would be irreproachable that was not modelled after an archetypal and intelligible idea. So when he willed to create this visible world, he first formed the intelligible world, so that he might employ a pattern completely Godlike and incorporeal.[17]

Tertullian appeals more to Stoic ideas:

> Even your own philosophers agree that the Logos, that is, Word and Reason, seems to be the maker of the universe. This Logos Zeno

16. Middle Platonism led also to the Neoplatonism of Plotinus, a third-century revival of Platonism supported by the Emperor Julian as a Hellenic substitute for Christianity. Ammonius Saccas, the Alexandrian from whose work it derived, was at one time an active member of the Alexandrian Christian school and reportedly a contemporary of both Origen and Arius.

17. Philo of Alexandria, *The Contemplative Life, the Giants, and Selections,* trans. D. Winston (Paulist, 1981), p. 99. Cp. E. R. Goodenough, *An Introduction to Philo Judaeus* (Blackwell, 1962); H. A. Wolfson, *Philo,* 2 vols. (Harvard Univ. Press, 1948); and Henry Chadwick, in Armstrong, ed., *The Cambridge History of Later Greek and Early Medieval Philosophy,* ch. 8.

[the Stoic] defines as the maker who formed everything according to a certain arrangement, the same Logos (he says) is called Destiny, God, the Mind of Jupiter, and the inevitable Fate of all things. Cleanthes combines all these predicates with Spirit which, according to him, permeate the Universe. Moreover, we too ascribe Spirit as its proper substance to that Word, Reason, and Power by which, as we have said, God made everything.[18]

But Tertullian accepts the idea of a two-stage Logos akin to Philo's: the Logos before creation as the wisdom of God, and the Logos as the immanent power within creation.[19]

Justin Martyr, however, follows the Platonists when he asserts that God created everything in his goodness out of shapeless matter, and he speaks approvingly of Plato's saying that God is the One. He admits that "when we say that God created and arranged all things in this world, we seem to repeat the teachings of Plato."[20] Clement of Alexandria claims that creation "tuned into concert the discord of the elements, that the whole universe might be in harmony," and he speaks of "the Logos, son of the *Nous* which is the Father."[21] Origen likewise affirms:

> . . . that God gave command about the vast things in the world and they were created, and that he who received the command was the divine Logos.[22]

Yet he disagrees with Plato over the eternality of matter and of uncreated souls, for nothing exists that has not received its existence from God.[23]

The Logos then is God's intermediary in creating and governing the universe, as middle Platonism proposed. But difficulties presented themselves. The two-stage Logos of Philo and Tertullian, while accepted by Justin and Clement, was unacceptable to Origen. If before creation the Logos existed only as the totality of wisdom in God's mind, and if

18. *Apology,* xxi.10.

19. *Against Praxeas,* vi. Cp. H. A. Wolfson, *The Philosophy of the Church Fathers,* I.45, 73-74.

20. *First Apology,* xx; *Exhortation to the Greeks,* xxii.

21. *Exhortation to the Greeks,* i; *Stromateis,* iv.

22. *Contra Celsum,* II.31.

23. *On First Principles,* I.3.

at creation the Logos gained personal existence by being emitted into the world like a spoken Word that brings order out of chaos, then matter is chaotic and a material creation has no inherent value after all. Moreover, the Logos would be neither co-eternal with God nor fully divine, but rather himself a created being. The ambiguous relation of the Logos to Plato's One carried over to the relation of Jesus Christ to the biblical God, and precipitated an extended christological con-troversy in the early church.

This controversy involved two questions. First, the two-stage theory of the Logos, implied by Plato and made explicit in Philo, was essentially taken for granted by Tertullian, Justin Martyr, and Clement of Alexandria. The Logos then is not an eternal being. On the other hand, Irenaeus and Origen maintained a one-stage theory, claiming that the Logos was generated from eternity. They prevailed, but in doing so posed a second question — whether the eternal generation of the Logos was a necessary overflow of the divine being (a position taken by Ammonius Saccas and later Neoplatonists), or whether it was by an act of God's free will. Arius took the latter view, claiming that there was a time when the Logos was not and that he was created by God out of nothing.

The resultant "Arian controversy" revealed that both alternatives led to the same result: whether the Logos was an emanation or a separate creation, he was not fully God but a subordinate being. Athanasius's solution, which the church finally adopted at the Council of Nicea in 325, was to find a third option, that the generation of the Logos was neither a necessity for God, as if he lacked something or was in some way deficient, nor an act of will. Rather, God is generative by nature: it is in the very being of God that the Logos is eternally the divine Son. As the Nicene Creed puts it, he is "very God of very God; begotten not made, being of one substance with the Father."

The christological controversy arose from debate about whether the material creation is good. For if the Logos was either generated or created to order an otherwise chaotic world, then the Gnostics were essentially correct and the good has no intrinsic basis in the nature of things. But if the Logos is eternally and fully God, equal with the Father, and if he brought the entire creation into being *ex nihilo,* rather than shaping preexistent and recalcitrant matter, then the entire creation and even matter bears witness to its maker and his purposes, and that is good.

Summary

A distinction therefore begins to emerge among three views of the relation between God and creation that we now identify as dualism, pantheism, and theism. The dualist echoes the Gnostic claim that matter exists independently of God, and that while it needs order and control it is itself uncreated. The pantheist pursues the Stoic and Neo-platonist direction that sees the material world, along with everything else, as emanating from the divine being and essentially one with it. The theist, on the other hand, distinguishes God from nature: God is self-existent, but nature is given existence as well as order by God's free act of creating. For the dualist, the creation is shaped *ex materia;* for the pantheist it emanates *ex deo;* for the theist it is an *ex nihilo* creation. The dualist regards matter itself as devoid of positive worth and the source of evil. The pantheist sees evil as an inevitable lack in finite things, a privation unavoidably inherent in their finiteness. For the theist, however, the fact that God gives order in giving existence undercuts the Gnostic dualism of material existence and rational order, while *ex nihilo* creation means that evil is not an inherent necessity of finite existence. The way is then open for a Christian view of good and evil such as Augustine spelled out more fully in the context of a Logos doctrine akin to that adopted by his predecessors, and so for the fuller development of a Christian position on fact and value.

CHAPTER FIVE

Augustine: God and the Soul

As WITH EARLIER Christian writers, the problem of evil was a major factor in drawing Augustine towards Platonism. In the *Confessions* he recounts his quest for happiness, the inner struggle with evil in his own soul, and the initial attraction of Manicheism's Gnostic-like philosophy. Manicheism traced the struggle between good and evil back before the constitution of the world, to a time when light and darkness were separated, creating two realms locked in eternal conflict. That conflict now goes on in human nature, for we each have two lives, two corporeal souls, the one a fragment of light, of the very substance of the good god, while the other springs from the intercourse of demons. These forces of darkness have imprisoned the light of the rational soul in a body; both good and evil are regarded as corporeal, and evil is described as "a foul and misshapen mass" devoid of reason or form.[1]

Even before his conversion Augustine had found insurmountable problems in such a view. Manicheism posed a dilemma:[2] either God generated the darkness or he did not. If he did, then it cannot have a different nature from his own; it is of the very nature of God, and is therefore really light and good. If God did not generate it, then it was

---

1. See Augustine's *Concerning Two Souls, Against the Manicheans; Confessions,* V.10.

2. *Against the Epistle of Manicheus called Fundamental,* ch. 25, in *A Select Library of the Nicene and Post-Nicene Fathers,* ed. Philip Schaff, vol. 4; *St. Augustine: The Writings Against the Manicheans and Against the Donatists* (first published 1887; Eerdmans, 1956).

made of some other nature, either good or evil. If good, then there is another eternal good than God; if evil, then good and evil are both eternal. In either case an eternal dualism limits God and makes him subject to its necessities; and as composites of both realms humans are made by demons, not by a God who is good. We are but pawns in the battle, with no real will of our own. As Augustine recognized, this eternal dualism allows no room for the eventual vindication of good, and any idea of cosmic justice is a delusion.

Augustine confesses that he was initially attracted to Manicheism because he as yet knew neither that God was a spirit rather than a corporeal being, nor that evil was a privation of good rather than an existent entity itself. It was Platonism, in all probability the Neoplatonism of Plotinus, that taught him these things and thereby provided an alternative to Manichean dualism.[3]

Plotinus was born in Egypt, studied in the Alexandrian school under Ammonius Saccas, and subsequently lived, taught, and wrote in Rome. Although his advice on practical matters was valued, he detached himself entirely from public affairs, preaching withdrawal from the world and cultivating a contemplative and somewhat mystical life. His religion was inward and individual, the solitary journey of the mind to God rather than a social or ceremonial activity. He reportedly refused even to sit for a painter or sculptor, because he saw no reason to leave posterity "an image of the image" in which nature had enclosed him. On his deathbed he said he was striving "to give back the divine in myself to the divine in the All."[4] These attitudes reflect his rejection of the materialism of his day, whether Epicurean or Stoic, and they reveal his firm belief that evil is due to the effect of bodily existence on the human soul. Sharing Plato's concern for the improvement of the soul, he builds his philosophy on what Middle Platonism had already done. But as Joseph Katz points out, he was less concerned with the interrelation of Plato's ideas or the architecture of his own system than with its reference to the human experience of good and evil.[5] This is doubtless what appealed to Augustine.

3. *Confessions*, III.7; VII. Cp. *City of God*, IX; X.1-3.

4. Porphyry's "Life of Plotinus," in *Plotinus: The Ethical Treatises*, trans. S. MacKenna (The Medici Society, 1926), pp. 1-2.

5. J. Katz, *Plotinus' Search for the Good* (Columbia Univ. Press, 1950), p. vii. Cp. R. Wallis, *Neoplatonism* (Scribner's, 1972), p. 47.

For Plotinus, the experience of the human soul, including the experience of evil, is a microcosm of being as a whole. The rational soul is arrested by the body, allured by its pleasures and enslaved by its vicissitudes. Life becomes fragmented. Freedom of will and independence of mind are lost. Desire, anger, and disorder, along with evil images and mistaken reasoning, haunt our lives. Animals devour one another, and humans attack each other. All is war without rest, without truce. Matter drags us down. We are prevented by our own nature, by accident or alien influence, from pursuing with undivided love what ought to absorb our best. Sometimes our self-will misleads us. A hasty first step goes uncorrected and ends up as a fixed but unchosen habit. Far too often, the senses misdirect us towards things inappropriate to the soul, for sensations are nothing but obscure thoughts, defective in form and lacking in reason. Plotinus's entire account treats evil as a disorder, a privation of form and the good; and in Augustine's mind it rang true.

Plotinus explained the soul's divided loyalty by ascribing to it a twofold nature, not in the dualistic, Manichean sense, but suggesting rather that the soul has two orientations, one lower and one higher. The lower is the life of the embodied individual, the seat of affections, of physical activity and sensations, much like Aristotle's passive intellect. The higher contemplates eternal forms, like the active intellect in Aristotle's scheme. Evil occurs when the soul descends to the lower level, where the light of intellect is obscured by the material objects we desire. As they dull the light in the soul, the will grows weaker until it is overthrown by ignorance or desire. The soul is then no longer master of itself, no longer free, but at the mercy of a changing world.[6]

Between these two levels of experience lies a third level: the guiding spirit of discursive reasoning that brings the light of the forms to bear on the world of sense, desire, and memory. Plotinus therefore has a way of salvation — a ladder from lower to higher levels of experience. If the soul is to return to its proper abode, it must first withdraw from the body, especially from earthly passions and desires, retaining only those pleasures and activities that are necessary to life and work, like food and drink and sex. Even these must be strictly regulated by reason,

---

6. *Enneads,* I.1, 8; III.2, 4 in MacKenna, *Plotinus: The Ethical Treatises.* See also A. H. Armstrong, ed., *The Cambridge History of Later Greek and Early Medieval Philosophy* (Cambridge Univ. Press, 1967), ch. 14.

if the soul is to be freed. The virtues of temperance, courage, and justice are needed — civic virtues that set bounds to desire and give beauty to the earthly life. For God such virtues are unnecessary; he has no passions to control, no lower soul. He is beyond virtue and goodness. To be like God, we too must rise beyond virtue.[7]

Virtue is, however, essential in the return of the soul; so too is knowledge. Since sense experiences present us only with changing images of shadows in Plato's cave, the soul must turn to dialectic and contemplate the forms of things in the light of eternal truth. The musician must distinguish physical harmony from its source in Beauty itself. The lover must love the form of Beauty independently of any physical image. We must give up the world of sense and settle in the intellectual realm of existence. If peace of mind were the goal, this would be enough. But living the good life means living with the greatest possible fullness. Ultimate happiness is to be found neither in bodily experiences nor intellectual vision, but in becoming like God — a completely self-sufficient, independent being. And that experience is possible only in union with God himself.[8]

Underlying this account of human experience is Plotinus's metaphysics, in which the soul is a microcosm of the whole. He is an idealist; for him, an immaterial World Soul is the underlying reality of the entire sensory realm. Bare matter has no being; devoid of form, it has no properties of its own, neither mass nor extension, nor any means of manifesting itself. It is nonbeing: formless, lawless, orderless, like the empty Receptacle of Plato's *Timaeus*, but it receives seeds of the World Soul that are capable of growing into every variety of physical manifestation. These seeds are the souls of people and other bodily things, the forms of individuals as well as classes.[9]

The lower cosmos, then, is far from self-sufficient, for it depends entirely on the higher. Within this higher realm are three ascending levels of being, three "hypostases." The first and lowest is the level the soul knows in itself, as giving life, movement, and order to things. It is the World Soul from which seminal souls emanate, and it has a double orientation: an inward vision of its own identity, function, and purpose; and an outward creativity that animates bodies and generates

---

7. *Enneads,* I.1.ii.
8. *Enneads,* I.1.iii-vii.
9. *Enneads,* I.8, II.4-5, III.6.

an ordered life like its own. An overall teleology thus pervades even the lower cosmos, for each individual soul likewise has inward vision and outward action. There is a twofold drive: one inward and upward towards the source and goal of all being, the other outward and downward into physical things. As Emile Brehier puts it,

> the soul of the world is then like a spiritual sea in which the sensible [soul] bathes; it is not like a workman who recollects, computes and plans.[10]

It is a living, creative whole that disperses in order to generate a lower world that still images the higher realm from which it came. Yet the World Soul is not self-sufficient; it too images that from which it emerged.

The individual soul contemplates ideal forms and applies them in the world of particulars. But Plotinus goes further than this, seeing forms interrelated in the unity of a conceptual whole. The whole sensible world is seen as having one eternal archetype, and to this Plotinus gives Anaxagoras's name, *Nous*. This is the second hypostasis in the immaterial, higher realm of being. From it all order and intelligibility flow, in both the world of thought and the world of outward action, the former by virtue of rational souls and the latter through those soul-seeds from which physical bodies spring. Plotinus uses the Stoic term *logoi spermatikoi* for these seminal forms. Their individualized natures all contribute to the one harmonious activity of God. "Do but survey the cosmos," he writes, and this is what you will hear:

> I am made by God: from that God I came perfect above all forms of life, adequate to my function, self-sufficing, lacking nothing.[11]

The world is a stage with many players and many parts to play; actors who "die" are not really dead, but merely change their costumes and take on other roles. They have their exits and their entrances, acting both grief and joy, and all of them work together for the good of the whole. The diversity and seeming disarray of this life contribute,

10. *The Philosophy of Plotinus,* trans. J. Thomas (Univ. of Chicago Press, 1958), p. 60. Cp. *Enneads,* IV.3, VI.7.
11. *Enneads,* III.2.iii.

then, to the harmony of the whole, for the universe echoes the rationality of *Nous*. What is evil to the individual soul always serves the greater good.[12]

Being, therefore, is good. Reality is value-laden throughout, and cosmic justice still exists. A. O. Lovejoy finds here a "Principle of Plenitude," an overflowing creative goodness that produces every conceivable degree of being and goodness, along with their every possible privation, which exists in such splendid completeness that every part contributes to the beauty of the whole.[13] But, says Plotinus, only a compound can be beautiful, for it takes harmony and symmetry and measure of the parts to produce the unity of the whole. Goodness or virtue is also a composite, a proper ordering of the parts of one's life and soul. While beauty and goodness, then, refer to *Nous,* which is the unity of all forms, they cannot be ascribed to unity in and of itself alone, the One.

The One is the highest and most ultimate level of the three eternal hypostases. It alone experiences what human souls seek, a self-sufficient identity that is independent and free, for it is oriented only inwardly to itself and not in the least outwardly in action towards any other. With no divided attention, no dualities, it is the ideal goal, the final cause towards which our souls and everything else strives. It is tied to nothing, yet everything is bound to it: it is the Unmoved Mover, the source of all goodness, order, and beauty; yet beyond them all. From its perfect unity emanates *Nous*, the unity of contemplative thought; from *Nous* in turn the World Soul emanates, with its ordered unity of outward activity; from the World Soul emanate individual souls, *logoi spermatikoi,* each giving a unity of individual identity, form, and disposition. From the One we emanate, and to the One we return. The result is a hierarchy of being and oneness, with corresponding degrees of beauty, goodness, and truth.

This is why detachment from particular bodily desires and involvements is the first necessary step to improving one's soul and knowing the good. Equally necessary is contemplation of the unity of forms in the

---

12. In a superb extended passage (III.2) Plotinus elaborates his metaphor of the play and players, anticipating Shakespeare's more famous use of the same idea. But Plotinus is dealing with the problem of evil, not just stages in life.

13. See A. O. Lovejoy, *The Great Chain of Being* (Harvard Univ. Press, 1936).

goodness, truth, and beauty of *Nous*. But a further step remains, one that transcends all awareness of the soul's individual identity. All separateness must go, even the difference between oneself and the objects of our thought. Intellect too is dismissed, along with everything that separates or even distinguishes the individual from the source of all being — the One. What remains is the vision that surrounds and immerses the soul as it loses itself in the all-transcending One.

It is a passing experience, Plotinus admits. "Falling back, we waken the virtue within until we know ourselves all order once more; once more we . . . move by virtue towards the Intellectual Principle," and on again to the One. This is where happiness is found, in liberation from corporeal things and the evil they bring.[14]

This then was the philosophy Augustine turned towards after his disillusionment with Manicheism. In an extended discussion of Greek philosophers in *The City of God*, he spells out what he came to appreciate. God is not like changing, corporeal things, for their unchangeable forms can only exist through one who is unchangeable, the eternal cause of all that exists. The individual mind therefore sees everything in relation to God, the source of understanding as well as of our being. Happiness, finding the good, is in knowing and loving God. Two things therefore concerned Augustine most of all: to know God and to know the soul. Knowing the former is essential to happiness. Knowing the latter can prepare us for it.[15]

But even Plato and the Platonists proved not entirely satisfactory, and in the *Retractiones* Augustine moderated his initial enthusiasm about them. Yet what he says about the soul still sounds quite Platonic. How can the soul be a corporeal thing when it embraces vast reaches of space, when it discerns truth from falsehood without reference to sense experience, and when it grows by learning rather than by just growing with the body? And if an immaterial soul is the seat of reason, must not a perfectly rational God be immaterial too? Moreover, since the soul gives life to the body, it cannot itself lack life; it controls the body, not by being spatially diffused through it (as the Stoics supposed) but by its life-giving attention to every part: a physical sensation is a temporary increase in the intensity of

14. *Enneads*, VI.9.xi. The sixth *Ennead* is devoted almost entirely to the One and the soul's reunion with it.

15. *City of God*, VIII.iv-xi. Cp. *Confessions*, VII.

the soul's influence in some particular place. Moreover, since the soul possesses life but is incorporeal, it must be independent of both bodily change and the body's death: it is immortal, and as such can find eternal happiness.[16]

[In one of his earliest writings, *On the Good Life,* Augustine argues that happiness is possessing what the rational soul most wants, namely truth and wisdom. Since God is perfect and eternal wisdom, what the soul most wants is God] Happiness is knowing him who is the Truth, the divine Logos. In *The City of God* he finds other concepts of the good too anthropocentric, as if the highest good were in oneself. The soul within is surely the chief good of the body, but it draws one beyond the self to something unchangeable and eternal. According to Augustine, we cannot escape this teleology. [As the opening paragraph of the *Confessions* affirms, "Thou hast made us for thyself, O God, and our hearts are restless until they find rest in thee."]

While this sounds much like Plotinus, Augustine breaks with both him and the Manicheans over the role of intellect in the improvement of the soul. In his own experience, he found that passions were not overcome by either dialectical or contemplative reason. We are not ruled by what we know but by what we most love. We are saved not by knowledge but by the love of God that moves the will. The gospel led him to part company with the Greeks.

Platonism talked of love as desire *(eros)* for either higher or lower goods, so that the love of wisdom underlies knowledge and virtue too. Augustine concurs, distinguishing love for things eternal *(caritas)* from disordered love *(cupiditas)* for temporal things. But the problem with this lower love is not simply that the mind's attention has been arrested by material things, as Plotinus claimed, but that we misdirect our desires. It is not the body that is evil, for the soul's self-love can be evil too; neither body nor soul is the soul's highest good.[17] Evil is due, rather, to disordered love willfully misdirected. The intermediary between the higher and lower aspects of the soul that directs us to things

---

16. *De Ordine,* II.11, 18; *Against the Epistle of Manicheus Called Fundamental,* xv-xix; *On the Measure of the Soul,* xix, xxii. Cp. *On the Immortality of the Soul.* See also E. Gilson, *The Christian Philosophy of St. Augustine* (Vintage Books, 1967), ch. 3.

17. *Confessions,* X.xxx-xli; *City of God,* XIV.iii-vii.

above is therefore not intellect nor dialectic, as Plotinus had said, but is rather a good will.[18]

Here we have the ingredients for an explanation of evil that became the classic point of reference in later Christian thought. First, Augustine agrees with Platonism and the Greek tradition in affirming that the natural order is good. Everything that exists, both corporeal and incorporeal, has form, and form is good. Absolute evil cannot exist, for to lack good altogether it would have to lack all form and could therefore not exist. Evil is then not something independent of the good as Manicheism taught, but simply a privation of form and so a lack of good. In the darkness there is always some light, and where corruption exists something good must first exist to be corrupted. A rotten apple is bad because it is losing the form of a good apple, and when it has altogether rotted away the apple no longer exists. Second, evils are only allowed within the limits of order, and so are made to serve a greater good. The apple that rots seeds the ground. The flea that bites is still a thing of beauty, its parts marvelously fitted and formed together. Even cockfighting exhibits the beauty of nature in the adept movements of contestants and the proud crowing of a victor. Nothing occurs outside the range of order, and within the hierarchical order of creation every-thing has its place.[19]

But Augustine goes beyond Plotinus's account in three regards. First, he ascribes the evils of the soul to the free choice of a will that deserts what is supremely good for lesser goods, and so distorts the natural order. Second, since the body is good, no neglect or abuse of it can be allowed. Temperance must be cultivated, and the harmony of a well-ordered life sustained by careful practice. Physical tempta-tions arise, but it is not the body that drags us into sin. Gradually a more positive view of material things emerged in Augustine's mind, and supplanted the negative view of Plotinus. Third, it is not knowing the good that overcomes evil in the soul but a free and full love for God.

18. *On Free Will*, 1; see also Robert E. Cushman's insightful essay, "Faith and Reason," in Roy Battenhouse, ed., *A Companion to the Study of St. Augustine* (Oxford Univ. Press, 1955), pp. 287-314.

19. This is the thesis of *De Ordine*, I, and *The Nature of the Good*. See also *Confessions*, VII, XII.i-xiii; *City of God*, XII.ii-viii; *Against the Epistle of Manicheus called Fundamental*, xx-xli; *Eighty-Three Disputed Questions*, q. 6.

Behind these differences from Platonism lies a more fundamental difference over the relation of God to the universe. Augustine applauds the Platonists for recognizing that God is the author of all things, the source both of the form that makes every changeable thing what it is and of the light of truth. But he plainly rejects the theory of emanation in favor of *ex nihilo* creation.[20] Nature is not an overflow of divine being, nor in any sense is it divine. The pantheistic tendency in both Neoplatonism and Stoicism is rejected as ridiculous.

> Granted that God is the World Soul, and that the world is the body of that soul, . . . it follows that nothing is left over which is not part of God. . . . Whatever any man tramples on is a part of God! And whenever any animal is slain, a part of God is slaughtered! . . . But they argue that only rational animals, such as men, are parts of God . . . then part of God gets a whipping when a boy is whipped? . . . parts of God become lewd, wicked, impious and utterly damnable.[21]

The Lord our God is not heaven and earth, but the one who freely chose to make heaven and earth.[22]

For Plotinus, moreover, the One can have no direct dealings with human beings, and cannot even be defined. A whole hierarchy of intermediary beings is required, yet even then only a few wise ones who withdraw from bodily life can, by strenuous effort, find God as in a sudden flash of dazzling light. But, Augustine responds, God does have direct dealings with us, and the only intermediary we need came to us in his Incarnation.[23]

The fact that God chooses to create *ex nihilo* gives human beings a separate existence with wills of their own. The free choice of the will is therefore possible for Augustine, whereas it was not for Plotinus. God, he says:

---

20. On his doctrine of creation see *On the Literal Meaning of Genesis*, discussed by Vernon J. Bourke in ch. XII of *Augustine's Quest for Wisdom* (Bruce Publishing Company, 1945). See also William Christian in ch. 12 of Battenhouse, ed., *Augustine*.

21. *City of God*, IV.xii-xiii. In book VIII he discusses at length the Platonist philosophy.

22. *City of God*, IV.xxx.

23. *City of God*, IX.xvi.

manages everything that he created in such a way as to allow each creature to initiate and carry through its own movements. For although they can do nothing without him, they are not what he is.[24]

The proper functioning of the human soul therefore involves free choice. Yet because God created all things freely and wisely, he also has foreknowledge of the causal processes operative in his creation, and is able to continue acting as he will. He therefore knows what is and is not within the power of our wills, and is able to influence them as he chooses. He can free the will from disordered love, preparing it to choose the highest good, God himself.[25] Augustine's doctrine of creation is thus at the basis of both his value theory and his theology of grace.

Neoplatonic influence is also evident in Augustine's theory of forms, yet here too it is Christianized. The forms are ultimately ideas in God's mind, *rationes aeternae,* intelligible archetypes of the entire created order. Plotinus found their unity in Intelligence *(Nous),* while Augustine follows the Alexandrian Christians and speaks of the Logos as the wisdom of God by whom all things were made and who became incarnate, "full of grace and *truth.*" In contrast to *Nous,* the Logos is both eternal and coequal with the Father, fully God. To know the Logos incarnate, Jesus Christ, is therefore to know God.

But the *rationes* were implanted by God in the original act of creation as hidden seeds *(rationes seminales)* that would later produce the rich variety of things that fill the created order, each species according to its own kind. They are developmental principles embedded in the original elements with potential to be actualized in the course of time. By this means God structured his creation as if by unchanging laws. What we call laws of nature are, by virtue of the *rationes,* manifestations of an eternal law, and so the order God created was itself good.[26]

Augustine accordingly finds more value in material things than did the Neoplatonists. He shows a deep appreciation of physical beauty, and disagrees with Porphyry that we should flee from all things sen-

---

24. *City of God,* VII.xxx. Cp. *Confessions,* XI.v.

25. *City of God,* V.ix; *Retractiones,* I.viii.

26. See especially *De Ordine.* Also *City of God,* XI.xvi-xxi; XII.i-viii; *Literal Meaning of Genesis; Eighty Three Disputed Questions,* q. 46. Cp. John 1:1-18.

sual.[27] In *On Christian Doctrine* he speaks at length about the values of liberal learning. Christians should not shun either music or literature just because the pagan gods were said to have invented them. Nor should they ignore matters of justice because pagan temples have been dedicated to it. Truth is of the Lord wherever we find it — in science, mathematics, history, or art.

> If those who are called philosophers, especially the Platonists, have said things that are indeed true and are well accommodated to the faith, they should not be feared; rather what they have said should be taken from them as from unjust possessors and converted to our use . . . like Israel spoiling the Egyptians. . . .[28]

Concerned always for the improvement of the soul, Augustine warns that while love edifies, knowledge puffs up; and some of what we need to know can be found only in Scripture.[29] We acquire knowledge, then, not only by reason but also by authority, both divine and human. In order of time, authority comes first, as in the instruction of children; but in the order of reality, since the *rationes* underlie everything in the created order, reason is prior. In knowing, we seek consistency and order by distinguishing and connecting, by analyzing and synthesizing the things we learn. Love for truth is a yearning for ordered unity — both in the soul and in the worlds of sense and thought. We love truth, but truth is no more a human creation than are moral values; nor is human reason autonomous, since the laws of valid inference, like order itself, are instituted by God in the order of creation.[30] Augustine accordingly finds objective grounds in the nature of God and creation for both truth and goodness. Beauty too derives from God, for in giving form to material creation he gave it the unity, proportion, and harmony that we recognize and love.

Sense perception alone, with its focus on changing particulars, is an inferior kind of reason that does not satisfy this love. Memory is a

---

27. *Retractiones*, I.4.

28. *On Christian Doctrine*, II.xl. *Retractiones*, I.4, corrects an earlier suggestion (*Soliloquies*, I.2) that none but the pure know truth, because in fact "others than the pure know many truths."

29. *On Christian Doctrine*, II.xli.

30. *On Divine Providence*, II.ix, xi, xviii; *Against the Academicians*, III.xx; *On Christian Doctrine*, II.xxxii.

kind of inner sense that looks within the soul, reflecting on both images from one's past and on truths that have been learned. But Augustine plainly rejects Plato's theory of recollection — that eternal truths are innate to the soul and recovered by dialectic. A temporal soul cannot by itself engender eternal truths; the Logos, the source of all form, is also the source of truth, a teacher who teaches within the soul by illumining the mind to see the beauty of eternal truth. This is not simply a process of recollection, nor does the soul gain direct insight into *rationes aeternae* in the mind of God. Rather, as the soul reflects on its perceptions and contemplates the created order, *rationes aeternae* come into view in the light of the Logos. This is not a special grace imparted to believers only; in the words of the apostle John, it is the light that lights all who come into the world. Immutable truth can be glimpsed by everyone, pagan or Christian, educated or otherwise. As the earlier church fathers said, all truth is ultimately God's truth, and all knowledge of truth may be accepted as such, regardless of where it is found.[31]

But knowledge, Augustine tells us, is not the highest good; God is. From the visible works of creation we can see the invisible attributes of God, for knowing the *rationes* in the creation leads us to that in which all truth exists. God is truth, as well as beauty and the good. The love of truth, beauty, and goodness, then, all draw the soul toward God.[32]

How can this be? God is the good, the highest good, and virtue is perfect love for God. But loving God does not exclude loving anything else, for if God loves his creation so should we. We should love physical beauty to the praise of the Creator, however, and not as the highest good in itself; this would be sin. To use physical pleasures rightly is good. Marriage, for instance, is both a vehicle for procreation and the means by which a man and woman are joined in mutual fidelity. But it is also a sacrament that celebrates the love and faithfulness of God, and thus points beyond itself.[33]

Love for God, then, is the inclusive, unifying virtue that brings life into proper balance and harmony. The other virtues are functions of love.

---

31. See *On the Trinity,* XII.1-2, 15; *Retractiones,* I.4, 8.

32. *Confessions,* IV.16; VII.17. Cp. *On Immortality of the Soul,* i; *On the Spirit and the Letter,* xix.

33. *Retractiones,* I.41, 48.

Temperance is love keeping itself entire and incorrupt for God; fortitude is love bearing everything readily for God's sake; justice is love serving God only and therefore ruling all else well; prudence is love distinguishing between what helps it towards God and what might hinder it.[34]

Virtue is not acquired by faith alone, for the soul advances little by little to the most virtuous life under the guidance of reason also. As authority and reason are both required in the pursuit of truth, so in the pursuit of virtue both faith and reason are needed; in both endeavors reason seeks order and unity. Virtue is the ordering of a soul in harmony with the truth about the good life. Augustine advocates a twofold procedure, one regulating the life and the other directing one's studies. Young people should avoid the vices they are prone to, like gluttony, selfishness, and anger, while respecting authority, learning patience, and cultivating friendship — all this with God as the object of their worship, thought, and desire.[35]

Constantly aware of the contrast between two loves, one for God and the good, the other for lesser things, Augustine's *City of God* develops this theme in relation to history and human society. On the one hand, love for God is represented by Jerusalem and the church; on the other hand, the lower love, concupiscence, is represented by Babylon and Rome. If justice means giving to each his due, then no earthly city is ever just that fails to give God his due and love him as the highest good. But love for God includes love for justice, since justice is the proper ordering of the state.[36]

Augustine's political and social concerns go far beyond those of Plotinus, who sought to insulate himself from public life and civic affairs. For Plotinus, the world was infected with unreality; it has always existed, but time is a flux in which decisive events can never occur and the soul is incarnated again and again. History repeats itself in cycles without a goal. In vivid contrast to this, Augustine's understanding of creation *ex nihilo*, by the deliberate act of a God who remains active in his creation, affords both a more optimistic and a more realistic view. History is important, for it reflects and magnifies the struggle of good

34. *On the Morals of the Catholic Church,* xv.

35. *On Divine Providence,* II.viii, xix; *The Measure of the Soul,* xvi.

36. *City of God,* XIX.xxi. Cp. Alasdair MacIntyre, *Whose Justice? Which Rationality?* (Univ. of Notre Dame Press, 1988), ch. 9.

and evil in the human soul. Events can effect decisive changes. God acts in history as he does in the soul. For humans, things past no longer exist and things future do not yet exist, but to the eternal and timeless God nothing is past or future; all is now present. He knows the end from the beginning. And what he did in Jesus Christ and will do in the final judgment are the most decisive events for good in all of time.[37] Cosmic justice is a reality because God acts in history as well as in nature and our souls.

Augustine, then, is distinguished from the Manichean and the ꜱᴜᴍ Neoplatonist by his understanding of creation *ex nihilo,* with its implications for both human freedom and God's ongoing activity in creation. Manicheism, with its eternal dualism of good and evil, offered no such hope for either history or the human soul. Neoplatonist pantheism offers hope only to the elite soul with an intellectual capacity to know the *Nous* before losing its identity and history in union with the One.

But it was Plato, in effect, who started Augustine on the road to knowledge of unchanging good in contrast to the world of sensory things. In return, Augustine asks the Greek philosopher,

> if some great and divine man should arise to persuade the peoples that such things were to be at least believed if they could not grasp them with the mind, . . . would you not judge that such a man is worthy of divine honors?

Plato, he says, would reply that it could not be done except by one uniquely endowed with divine wisdom and virtue, who would have earned a place above all humanity. But Augustine continues: this very thing has come to pass, for such a one has come. The incarnate Logos has dwelt among us, full of grace and truth. If Plato could live his life again, he would become a Christian, as many Platonists had recently done.[38]

---

37. *City of God,* XI.iv-vi; *Eighty-Three Disputed Questions,* q. 17. See also William Christian, pp. 323-24, in Battenhouse, ed., *Augustine,* ch. 12. Charles Taylor's concern that Augustine stresses the logos-order of creation instead of God being the sovereign actor seems to overlook the freedom to act that this view of history provides for both God and the human soul. See *Sources of the Self* (Harvard Univ. Press, 1989), ch. 7.

38. *On True Religion,* iii.3-7.

In fact, not only did some Platonists find a fuller and more adequate account in Christianity and become Christians, but many Christians followed Augustine and became Platonists. It would be hard to exaggerate the widespread influence of this intellectual tradition during the Middle Ages. Some medieval thinkers missed the importance of Augustine's crucial distinction between *ex nihilo* creation and the theory of emanations. Some opted for an other-worldly mysticism, as if the creation were not at all good or beautiful and embodied no truth. The man who followed Augustine most fully was probably Anselm of Canterbury (d. 1109). A debate was in progress over the relation of reason to authority, more specifically of philosophy to theology. Some wanted to separate the two, confining dialectic to intellectual exercises for students. Berengar of Tours, meanwhile, insisted that authority alone is not sufficient in settling arguments. As a teacher of his fellow monks, Anselm like Augustine found dialectic helpful in understanding theological beliefs. Though he felt it was more than an intellectual exercise, he did not claim that it could demonstrate truth to unbelievers. He believed, rather, that dialectic aids faith seeking understanding; it clarifies truth and exhibits its reasonableness to the believer. In his writings, Anselm followed the monk's practice of interspersing prayers for illumination with his philosophical reflection.[39]

Anselm's theological understanding is itself cast in largely Augustinian form; that is, he assumes a hierarchy of beings, each with its own nature, in which God at the peak is the one "than which no greater can be conceived." God is the good, and since things are ordered by their forms, God is also truth. Granted this hierarchy, we can readily understand that God necessarily exists, because in an ordered universe there must be an objective ground for all degrees of being, goodness, and truth. Value must be grounded in fact.

---

39. *Sermon* CXXVI, in E. Przywara, *An Augustine Synthesis* (Sheed & Ward, 1945). On Anselm's view of faith and understanding in his historical setting, see Armstrong, ed., *The Cambridge History of Later Greek and Early Medieval Philosophy*, chs. 37, 38.

CHAPTER SIX

Thomas Aquinas:
A Creational Ethic

If Augustine's name is associated with Platonism, Aquinas's is associated with Aristotelianism. Indeed, his teacher, Albertus Magnus, had endeavored to make use of Aristotelian insights, and doubtless influenced Thomas in this direction. As Copleston puts it, "St. Albert was Thomas's Socrates."[1] But it was while he was teaching in Paris between 1268 and 1272, embroiled in controversy with Averroists like Siger de Brabant, that Aquinas developed his systematic use of Aristotle. The *Summa Theologica* was written mostly during this period, and the *Summa Contra Gentiles* immediately followed.

A century before Aquinas, the Moslem philosopher Averroes regarded Aristotle's work as the very culmination of human intellectual achievement. He interpreted Aristotle as holding to a hierarchy of being that stretched from God, who is pure actuality, to prime matter, which is pure potentiality, with ten created intelligences as intermediaries between the unity of God and the plurality of nature. Rather than creating the world *ex nihilo,* God draws the forms of things from the potency of uncreated matter. The tenth intelligence is a unitary active intellect that draws the passive intellects of human beings to intellectual acts; at death, however, the individual's active intellect is absorbed back into the unitary intelligence. Both the eternality of prime matter and

1. F. Copleston, *A History of Philosophy* (St. Martin's Press, 1950), vol. 2, p. 303.

57

this denial of individual immortality conflicted with Islamic theology, but Averroes claimed that while philosophy can clearly understand such things, theology expresses them allegorically to accommodate the ordinary person's less precise thinking.

Averroes's views, along with his attitude to theology, deeply troubled Christian thinkers. Yet Christian Averroists like Siger de Brabant believed the views to be rationally demonstrated. If faith affirms individual immortality, it must be that God miraculously individuates the rational soul, something that is impossible by natural means. A doctrine of twofold truth emerged: what is true in philosophy may be false in theology, and vice versa. Two contradictory assertions may both be true. Although Siger may later have renounced these Averroist views, they made Aristotle a highly controversial figure.

To Bonaventure, the Franciscan scholar and Aquinas's contemporary, either philosophy yields the truth or theology does; they cannot both do so when their "truths" contradict each other. Bonaventure opted for theology and rejected Aristotelian philosophy altogether. The problems arose, he contended, because Aristotle and the Averroists failed to philosophize, as Augustine did, in the light of faith; for without the illumination of faith, the truth cannot be found. Aristotle's God could not create because he thinks not about nature but only on his own thinking. In contrast, Augustine saw that with Platonic exemplars (forms) in mind, God can both affect things as a final cause, drawing out their inherent potentials, and as efficient cause create *ex nihilo*.

Moreover, since the exemplars are contained in the divine Logos, every created thing is in some way like God and the world as a whole should manifest his glory. But without the exemplars neither creation nor providence is possible, nor is human accountability to God in this life or the hereafter. It is not surprising, then, that by rejecting Plato's theory of ideas, Aristotle was led to the eternality of matter and the loss of individual immortality. So Bonaventure reaffirmed Augustine's exemplarism, along with a dualism of body and soul and a divine illumination.[2]

Although he conceded Aristotle's mistakes, Aquinas was not prepared to write him off as definitively as Bonaventure had done. Even a pagan philosopher, he believed, attains some truth if he elaborates a

2. For a fuller account of Bonaventure see Copleston, chs. 25-29, and Etienne Gilson, *The Philosophy of St. Bonaventure* (Sheed and Ward, 1938).

more or less satisfactory metaphysic, even though that metaphysic contains errors. Aquinas believed Aristotle had done this in his teleological metaphysics, in which God forms the world for an end. Aquinas opted to retain Aristotle's philosophy of nature while reintroducing Augustine's exemplarism, and to show that the resultant view of nature best supported a theology of creation and the human person. Aristotle's philosophy had to be refocused if it was to be pressed into service by Christian philosophers; but by repairing its internal difficulties, a far better metaphysics becomes possible, a metaphysics thoroughly consonant with Christian theology. But this could not be achieved — this rectifying of a Greek philosophy — without the aid of revelation.

Aquinas held that philosophy and theology, like reason and revelation, cannot ultimately contradict each other.[3] Reason by itself is limited when it starts with the natural world as Aristotle did; for the truths of revelation assented to by faith far exceed what reason alone can demonstrate. Faith's starting point is God — the supreme being, the highest good, and the highest object of thought. This was the new focus Aristotelianism needed; it could be demonstrated by reason, and would require the realignment of Aristotelian views concerning both nature and the human self.

Aristotle's ethic must first be infused with a new perspective, one that Aristotle himself had already pointed to: a person's proper end is no longer one's self, the actualization of human potential, but rather God. That end, moreover, is not achieved by natural means alone; it requires supernatural grace. Yet grace does not annul nature any more than faith annuls reason or theology annuls philosophy. They are mutually supportive: as faith infuses reason with new light, and theology gives philosophy new direction and brings it to completion, so grace infuses nature and, in bringing us to God, brings human nature to completion. Like Aristotle's supreme good, God is the all-inclusive end that makes all other goods possible: the divine *telos* is the basis for all other values.

Aristotle's conception of God was, as we have seen, somewhat hazy, and God's relationship to nature very limited. It is clear that an

3. *Summa Theologica*, I, q. 1; *Summa Contra Gentiles*, I.1-8. Arvin Vos, *Aquinas, Calvin, and Contemporary Protestant Thought* (Eerdmans, 1985), critiques some popular misconceptions. See also E. Gilson, *The Philosophy of St. Thomas Aquinas*, trans. E. Bullough, 2nd ed. (W. Heffer, 1929), ch. 2.

eternal Unmoved Mover exists who as final cause moves the heavenly spheres to emulate his own perfection. It is also clear that the Aristotelian God is the highest conceivable good fully actualized. But a Christian would be thoroughly dissatisfied with a God who is both unaware of anything other than his own thinking and unable to act on anything as efficient cause. Such a God — who could neither create, rule, nor redeem — is not the guarantor of good in and for the creation.

The development of topics at the outset of Thomas's *Summa Theologica* reveals his systematic attack on these issues. After an introductory discussion on the roles of faith and reason in relation to theology, he proceeds to establish his conception of God with reference to Aristotle's system, yet over and against it. While the first of his "five proofs" for the existence of God shows the necessity of a first mover for all natural motion, the second immediately concludes that the first mover is also the first *efficient* cause. The third demonstrates that God is a *necessary* being, self-existent, while the fourth argues that he is *the highest good,* as Augustine had claimed. The fifth argument, from the "governance" of the world, then adds that God must possess intelligence and knowledge to "direct" natural things to their end.[4] The conclusion is that God is the creator and does not just think on his own thinking, but knows his creatures and has their good in mind. The deficiencies in Aristotle's conception of God are thus repaired at the outset. In later discussions, Thomas goes on to elaborate on God's goodness and knowledge and active power; God is the efficient as well as the formal and final cause of all creation.

The idea of creation by the power of God was alien to the Greek mind and would have seemed impossible. For if God is perfect and needing nothing — pure act with no unrealized potency — why ever would he make anything else? A self-sufficient God would surely be satisfied in being himself and thinking about himself only. But if God is not the efficient cause of the world's being, then either its material must have existed eternally and some kind of dualism results, or else its very being emanates from the divine being, as the Neoplatonists aver. For Neoplatonists, God is the One who neither thinks about finite things nor acts in the world.

Aquinas goes further than both Aristotle and Plotinus in making God the source of our being as well as of goodness. The key is that

4. *S.T.,* I, q. 3.

God's very nature is to exist. As Etienne Gilson puts it, he is not a perfect essence that happens to exist, but the very essence of existence, the perfection of being itself, a *necessary* being who imparts existence as well as form in the act of creating.[5] He creates neither out of some co-eternal material nor out of his own being, but *ex nihilo*. He creates not only form but also matter itself — a notion the Greeks could not conceive of.

> Therefore as the generation of a man is from the not-being which is not-man, so creation, which is the emanation of all being, is from the not-being which is nothing.[6]

> Whatever is the cause of things considered as beings, must be the cause of things not only according as they are "such" by accidental forms, nor according as they are "these" by substantial forms, but also according to all that belongs to their being in any way whatever. And thus it is necessary to say that also prime matter is created by the universal cause of being.[7]

Creation, contrary to both Aristotle and Plotinus, is the knowing act of a personal God, creating freely from a whole range of possible things. While Aquinas follows Augustine's theological lead in this, he develops the idea more fully and in a different fashion. If every created thing is to participate in some way in God's being and goodness, then God knows created things through knowing his own essential nature. God's ideas of things are the exemplars, the formal cause of what he creates. But these exemplars have no separate existence like Plato's forms, nor are they just ideas of universals like species and genera. God knows and has a purpose for every particular thing in creation. God's ideas are thus of every particular combination of form and matter; however lowly its existence, even primal matter — by its pure potentiality — imitates in some degree the being of God. God's ideas therefore include species and individuals and particular qualities of every sort. He knows the individual nature of every created thing, both the substance and the accidents:

---

5. E. Gilson, *God and Philosophy* (Yale Univ. Press, 1941), ch. 2; cp. Patrick Madigan, *Christian Revelation and the Completion of the Aristotelian Revolution* (University Press of America, 1988).
6. *S.T.*, I, q. 45, art. 1.
7. *S.T.*, I, q. 44, art. 2.

as the active power of God extends not only to forms, which are the source of universality, but also to matter, . . . the knowledge of God must extend to singular things, which are individualized by matter.[8]

Since we hold matter to be created by God, though not apart from form, matter has its idea in God; but not apart from the idea of the composite, for matter in itself can neither have being, nor be known.[9]

Whatever is caused by God has its idea in God. Now, God causes not only substances but also accidents as well. Therefore accidents have an idea in God.[10]

All that occurs, then, draws on the power and wisdom and goodness of God, and is known by him.

So then this is the best possible world

God creates in accord with his ideas, selecting from all possible things what he will cause to exist. Only particular things can exist, and particulars are composed of form and matter. Because God draws each particular nature from the potentiality of matter, it is matter that individuates the particular, not some combination of forms or the privation of form. The form of a thing is then not just the form of its species, but the form of the particular substance with its individualized nature. Without this substantial form a particular could not exist as a particular at all. Of course, substantial forms are similar in all members of a species, so that we can think abstractly about the essence of the species; but the substantial form of an individual is the form of that individual being. Individuals have their own distinguishable natures by virtue of having individual existence per se.[11]

In receiving its own proper nature, every created thing has its own final cause, its appropriate good. In its own way and to its own proper degree, its being is like the being of God. Together, all created things are ordered as a universe that tells of its maker's perfect goodness and power. Each particular has its own "proximate" end that contributes to the ultimate end of glorifying God within the fullness of creation. Proximate and ultimate ends do not conflict, for each contributes to the other. God is thus the good by whose virtue anything else is good,

8. *S.T.,* I, q. 12, art. 11.
9. *S.T.,* I, q. 15, art. 3, reply obj. 3.
10. *On Truth,* q. 3, art. 7.
11. *S.T.,* I, q. 65, art. 3; *S.C.G.,* II.40.

the exemplar as well as the efficient and final cause. All being is good, with degrees of goodness depending on the degree to which the natural potential of a thing is actualized. Being and goodness, it turns out, while different in their meaning, refer to the same thing.[12] Value inheres in reality because goodness is one with the being of God, whose likeness is shared in by all creation. *Response to Euthyphro*

Since this is the case with creation, it is also true of humanity. Because our reason for being is not in ourselves, Aquinas rejects such claimants to highest good as wealth (a mere means, not an end), honor (the result of some good act, not itself the good), fame, power, bodily well-being, or pleasure. Our highest good is higher than all of these. It is beyond ourselves; it is God.[13] Human life should accordingly be understood in teleological fashion as having the continuity of a unified quest, like a story with a beginning, an unfolding plot, and an end.[14] We are led beyond bodily goods by asking what is the proper good of the soul. We are led beyond the passive intellect (needed for sense knowledge), and beyond even the active intellect (drawing knowledge from sense experience), to a contemplative knowledge of transcendent things — to God himself.

Yet Aquinas is careful to avoid a body-soul dualism that deprecates the body. The body is not a prison that limits the soul, for the soul needs the body as the instrument of its actions and the immediate source for its knowledge. The soul is united with the body as form united with matter. Contrary to Plato's dualism it has its being and its action only as embodied, for in bringing its powers to the potential of the body they become one substance and one act. Moreover, since the form is not a universal entity shared by every member of the species, but the substantive form of a particular individual, it has both universal qualities in common with the entire species and particular qualities proper to itself.[15] An individualized soul of this sort is capable of individual immortality, contrary to the Averroists for whom the soul is just universal form.

12. *S.T.,* I, q. 6, art. 3; q. 44, art. 4; *S.C.G.,* II.45; III.17-20; *On Truth,* q. 27, art. 1, 2. See Scott Macdonald, ed., *Being and Goodness* (Cornell Univ. Press, 1991).

13. *S.T.,* II-I, qq. 1-5; *S.C.G.,* III-I.27-37.

14. Gilson, *Philosophy of St. Thomas Aquinas,* p. 344; Alasdair MacIntyre, *Three Rival Versions of Moral Inquiry* (Univ. of Notre Dame Press, 1990), p. 197.

15. *S.C.G.,* II.56-73 (esp. 57 and 68).

Such is the reality in which Aquinas's ethic is grounded, a reality that includes the past, present, and future of the person as part of an entire creation manifesting the goodness of its maker. Unified selves, by virtue of their natural potential, have ends or virtues they are designed to pursue; these virtues constitute our likeness to God as particular beings. The image of God in all of us is what the entire species shares in common, an intellectual capacity that, along with other natural capacities, has its own proper ends.[16] But a moral likeness to God is more than this, and it too is grounded in the makeup of a human person.

To see this more fully, we must look more closely at Aquinas's psychology — pervaded like the rest of his metaphysic by an Aristotelian kind of teleology. By virtue of their fixed natures, things have natural inclinations towards certain ends. Nonsentient things are entirely determined in what they do, as in the case of a falling stone. Sentient things have appetites but no power to control or direct them, as with a physical reflex or an instinctual drive. But rational beings, having both sensory and intellectual powers, have the freedom to restrain their inclinations or direct them to known ends. Sensory inclinations are of two sorts: the concupiscible, which tend towards what is naturally pleasant, agreeable, or useful; and the irascible, which respond to difficulties, challenges, or hostility. The intellect, which apprehends whatever appears good or bad, inclines one towards or away from such objects, while the will is a rationally directed appetite for known ends and for the means towards them. The intellect is free regarding the act (to will or not to will), its object (to choose this or that), and its end — for it can even take something evil to be good if it appears so. While the will is moved by what the intellect proposes, it can also function as the efficient cause of both bodily action and other activities of the soul, even moving the intellect to consider what it does.[17]

The intention of the will is therefore crucial, and it must be properly informed by the intellect. Human nature provides for this by means of conscience, our capacity to make judgments about particular actions. Moral judgments, like other kinds of judgment, depend on first principles. The first principles of moral knowledge are evident

16. *S.T.,* I, q. 93.
17. *On Truth,* qq. 22, 24; *S.T.,* II-I, qq. 6-10. This emphasis on will represents Augustine's influence in Aquinas's adaptation of Aristotle's psychology.

when a natural mental habit (Aquinas calls it *synderesis*) reminds us that we should do good and avoid evil, or that we should live according to reason, or that God must be obeyed.

> Thus, the act of conscience is the result of a kind of syllogism. For example, if the judgment of synderesis expresses this statement: "I must not do anything which is forbidden by the law of God," and if the knowledge of higher reason presents this minor premise: "Sexual intercourse with this woman is forbidden by the law of God," the application of conscience will be made by concluding: "I must abstain from this intercourse."[18]

Conscience, then, provides a kind of knowledge that is not innate but, in good Aristotelian fashion, depends on first principles. Synderesis provides only the first principles, whether or not they are verbalized or merely implicit in our actions.

Plainly the minor premise in the above example calls for some knowledge of God's law, and Aquinas finds that such knowledge is available in two ways: the divine law given in Scripture and entrusted to the church, and the natural law that Paul speaks of as "written in the heart."[19] In his account of natural law, Aquinas points again to the first principle that good is to be done and evil avoided, and then shows how human nature provides knowledge of moral law. All beings have good ends to which they naturally incline. Self-preservation is a natural good for all animate beings, as are reproduction and the raising of offspring. Natural moral law includes all this for human beings, but adds the goods proper to distinctively rational beings, namely the ends of knowing the truth about God and living in an ordered society.[20] Since the natural order is teleological, oriented to good ends, moral law is evident in the natural ends of the human species.

Since we are by nature social beings, society is essential to the human good. Aquinas thus argues that human law properly derives from natural law. Jacques Maritain points out that we depend on society not only for material or intellectual needs; we also have a need to give — an inner openness that makes relationships possible. I cannot achieve my own good without subordinating myself to others in a common

18. *On Truth*, q. 17, art. 2; cp. q. 16, art. 1.
19. Rom. 2:14-15.
20. *S.T.*, II-I, q. 94, art. 2.

bond. Society exists, then, not ultimately for the individual's good, nor for the aggregate of individual goods, but for the common good of people living together in justice for all.[21]

The natural law is then derived from self-evident first principles known by the light of reason, implanted in us by God. The truth we see is a kind of reflected likeness of the uncreated truth — of eternal law, the wisdom of God himself.[22] We know the will of God by virtue of the fact that synderesis and natural law are natural "habits," a God-given potential for moral knowledge. A habit is literally something we "have," a disposition or inclination. Synderesis is a habit because it disposes us towards knowing moral law. Natural law is a habit because its precepts are sometimes "in the reason only habitually" (i.e., *potentially*) rather than consciously considered.[23]

Habits may incline the will towards either good or evil, and order actions well or otherwise. As a habit, synderesis provides only the seed of natural moral knowledge, and natural moral law is only seminally present in us until this moral knowledge is actualized. Good habits are developed, as Aristotle said, by repeated actions deliberately chosen. Virtues are good habits; vices are bad ones. Virtues are habits related to natural ends. Vices are contrary to nature.[24]

> Since habit measures the greater or lesser distance of the individual from his proper goal and causes him to conform more or less to his proper type, a careful distinction must be made between a habit disposing him to perform an act conforming to his nature, and one disposing him to an act in disagreement with his nature. The former are good habits, and such are also the virtues; the latter are bad habits, and these are vices.[25]

Like Aristotle, Aquinas distinguishes intellectual from moral virtues. The former relate to either speculative or practical reason, the latter to the appetites. But he goes beyond Aristotle in adding the theological virtues of faith, hope, and love, which direct us toward God. For according to natural law, knowing the truth about God is essential

21. *The Rights of Man and Natural Law* (Scribner's, 1943), ch. 1.
22. *On Truth*, q. 11, art. 1, reply.
23. *S.T.*, II-I, q. 94, art. 1.
24. *S.T.*, II-I, qq. 49-55.
25. Gilson, *The Philosophy of St. Thomas Aquinas*, p. 316.

to achieving the good.[26] Virtue, as disposition towards the good, is the right ordering of one's desires, and love for God should be the first and fullest of all desires.

Perfect goodness is to be found only in God; the love and knowledge of God — imperfect in our present lives — are perfected in the next. In the life we now live, divine grace can impart a fuller knowledge of God than the natural light of reason can attain by itself; but in the next life supernatural light will lift the intellect to the vision of God himself. As Copleston puts it, Aristotle's truly happy man is the philosopher, but for Aquinas the philosopher is too imperfect by far. The truly happy person is not the philosopher but the saint.[27] For the saint, every desire is fully satisfied — not by the contemplative wisdom Aristotle advocated, but by a beatific vision of the divine.

By integrating Augustine's theology with Aristotle's philosophy, the culmination of Aquinas's ethic is inescapably religious. Granted the premise that God created us for himself, our hearts remain restless until they rest in God. Aristotle's teleology simply provides the way of seeing how — knowingly or otherwise — we incline towards God. The good is grounded in the reality of God, and in who we are and shall be. The Greek vision of fact and value thus finds its fulfillment in Christian thought.

26. See Henry Veatch, *Human Rights, Fact or Fancy* (Louisiana State Univ. Press, 1985), p. 65.

27. Copleston, *History of Philosophy,* p. 398. See *S.T.,* I, q. 12: "How God Is Known by Us." See also *S.C.G.,* III.51-63.

CHAPTER SEVEN

Scotus, Ockham, and the Reformers: What God Commands

L OVE FOR G OD is so plainly given the highest place in both the Jewish and Christian Scriptures that a Christian ethicist could hardly disagree with the insistence of Augustine and Aquinas that it is indeed our highest end. This view of things did not change with the breakdown of the medieval synthesis. The metaphysical foundations of ethics, however, developed from early Greek concepts of cosmic order, were eventually rejected as part of the medieval synthesis of Christianity with Greek philosophy.

Some Protestants claim that Aquinas's distinction between philosophy and theology initiated the breakdown of this synthesis and prepared the way for the autonomy of reason asserted in the Enlightenment. Alasdair MacIntyre, on the other hand, traces the same break to Duns Scotus (1265?-1308).[1] Yet in fact it was William of Ockham who rejected the classical way of reasoning and developed a *via moderna*, rejecting the reality of universals and altogether changing the meaning of natural moral law. The Protestant Reformers show the influence of these changes.

The crucial difference between Aquinas and both Scotus and Ock-

---

1. Alasdair MacIntyre, *Three Rival Versions of Moral Inquiry* (Univ. of Notre Dame Press, 1990), pp. 152-57.

ham lies in their conception of God and his relation to creation. They all agree that God is a being of infinite perfection and the highest good of all creatures, that every existing thing manifests the goodness of God, and that rational beings should do so deliberately. They also agree that God never acts contrary to reason; his relation to his creatures is guided by right reason. But for Scotus and Ockham the will of God ultimately determines the nature of what he creates, and not the metaphysical necessity behind some immutable natural law. Since God is perfect, so too is his will. Since he never acts contrary to reason, his will is neither arbitrary nor capricious. God thus finds in himself the norm for his willing and acting. He knows and loves all good possibilities, and chooses from among them in relation to how the harmony of creation as a whole will manifest his perfection. God did not have to create, nor did he have to create this particular world. He chose to do so freely. Creation is not necessary but contingent, nor is there a sole intrinsically necessary hierarchical order that God must abide by in creating.

For Duns Scotus[2] this is because God, in choosing what to create, has direct knowledge of this particular creation. God knows individuals themselves, not just eternal exemplars of universal kinds and qualities. The distinction between form and matter is purely formal; they are not in reality separate entities, nor can individuality be separated from form and matter. Scotus claims that in creating an individual, God knows and wills the particular being it is, its generic form, its particular matter, and its this-ness *(haecceitas)*. The particular being is directly present in God's thought, as it is in ours.

Being, moreover, is the most general of all concepts and therefore the overall subject of metaphysics. It is a univocal concept applying in the same way to God and all his creatures, so that we can know that God exists in the same general sense as other things we know. The idea of degrees of being, in a hierarchy stretching from God all the way to the least and lowest, is thereby rejected. Various qualities like goodness and beauty may admit of degrees, but not being itself. It follows that creation

2. On Scotus, see Efren Bettoni, *Duns Scotus: The Basic Principles of His Philosophy*, trans. B. Bonansea (Catholic University of America Press, 1961); F. Copleston, *A History of Philosophy*, vol. 2 (St. Martin's Press, 1950); Allan B. Wolter, *The Philosophical Theology of John Duns Scotus* (Cornell Univ. Press, 1990).

3. *Duns Scotus, Philosophical Writings*, trans. Allan Wolter (Bobbs-Merrill, 1962), pp. 3-13.

is in every regard contingent rather than necessary. Nothing in God necessitated that he create, or that he create this particular order of things. No exemplars necessitated it, nor did some ideal hierarchy require this or that thing to fill up every possible degree of being and perfection. In effect, ours is only one of many "best possible" worlds. Creation and its laws are neither necessary nor immutable; only God is.

But God remains our highest end, and love of God is for Scotus the only act that of its own nature is always intrinsically right. Scotus's point is that if will, not intellect, is the highest human power, then the intention is morally more significant than the act itself; good intention towards God means loving and obeying him freely. Free will is therefore crucial to Scotus's thinking. But it is not just an intellectual desire to know God, nor an Aristotelian *telos* for self-fulfillment as an intrinsic necessity of our being. Free will rather is a will freed from bondage to emotions and desires so as to obey God freely.[4]

This is where the concept of natural law appears. Scotus tells us that it binds the conscience of all men regardless of time, place, custom, and mentality. Its substantial content is essentially the same as it was for his predecessors. Like Aquinas, he appeals to Romans 1 in support of the claim that natural law is humanly accessible. But where Augustine and Aquinas derive natural from eternal law and thus from divine reason, Scotus derives it from God's will, thus making room for more flexibility. Natural law is required not by an intrinsic order of nature but by God alone; and he in some circumstances might overrule contingent nature's laws.

Consider the decalogue as a statement of the law of nature. The first three commandments concern our relation to God, who by virtue of his very nature as the most perfect being should be loved above all else. To the first three commandments, then, there can be no exception and no change. Because God necessarily exists, this law of nature is logically necessary. But the last seven commandments, concerning our relations to other people, are contingent on whatever aspects of social existence they refer to. As such they are not absolute; God might call for an exception, as he did in allowing polygamy among Old Testament patriarchs, or in asking Abraham to sacrifice Isaac, or in commanding Hosea to marry a harlot. Our moral obligations, Scotus concluded, are not grounded unchangeably in the nature and value of created things, especially now

4. Wolter, *Philosophical Theology*, ch. 7.

that human existence and the creation we inhabit are so tainted by human sin. Our path lies between the fall and God's kingdom. We have not yet arrived, nor has our awareness of the law of nature progressed as it might have. As Old Testament moral practice was preparatory, our present moral understanding may also be provisional,[5] and for this reason God's actual commands to us may differ from the decalogue.

God's will is not always revealed in explicit commandments we can obey without further reasoning. We must often decide by means of right reason. Here Scotus reflects Aquinas's attention to the end or intention of an agent (final cause), the form or manner in which a deed is accomplished (formal cause), and the circumstances and persons involved (material cause).[6] The will, as efficient cause of any free moral choice, rightly acts with regard to all these considerations. But Scotus's voluntarism has changed the grounds of natural moral law, and opened the way to the emergence of Ockham's *via moderna*.

Ockham's interests were less speculative and metaphysical than those of Aquinas and Scotus, but his work was more analytic and critical. No less theological in his orientation, however, he was concerned to purge Christian thought of all Greek speculation that compromised the freedom and omnipotence of God. He therefore followed Scotus's voluntarism — a mark of Franciscan thought, in contrast to the Dominican emphasis on the divine intellect and eternal exemplars, which Ockham regarded as an intrusion into Christian thought of Greek necessitarianism.

Like Scotus, then, Ockham insisted on the contingency of creation. God did not have to create, nor was he bound by unchanging exemplars of genera, species, and universal qualities. He chose individual entities to create, and in doing so he chose this particular world order. Why then do we need Scotus's speculative principles to explain individuality? Ockham goes further than Scotus: realistic theories of universals must be rejected altogether.

To begin, God's ideas are not universal archetypes eternally present in the divine intellect; they are divinely created intellectual acts rather than mental objects. They do not always exist, but simply occur as God thinks of them. Further, the ideas according to which God acts are

5. Wolter, *Philosophical Theology*, p. 162.

6. C. R. S. Harris, *Duns Scotus* (Clarendon, 1927), vol. 2, ch. 8. Cp. Aquinas, *S.T.*, I-II, q. 18, arts. 4 and 5.

particular ideas of individuals and all their particular qualities, not ideas of genera, species, universal qualities and relations, plus what Scotus called the "this-ness" *(haecceitas)* of a particular. No universal idea of humanity exists in God's mind, nor any universal law of nature that is immutable in its essence. Rather, God knows every individual, every event, every act, for he has created those ideas, and insofar as the things they represent really exist, God concurs in them all. His will is sovereign.

Nor, according to Ockham, are there real universals in nature. If human nature were a form distinct from the individual Socrates, then it would not be Socrates' intrinsic essence. Socrates cannot be what really he is not. And if an incorruptible form informs the human body, then Socrates' body would not be corruptible. Marilyn Adams identifies three main weapons that Ockham uses against the theory of universals:[7]

1. The existence of any particular of a given species is logically independent of the existence of any other particular of that species. This denies Aquinas's view that all particulars of a given species have some common nature as one of their constituents.
2. Nothing can individuate or be individuated by being extrinsic to itself. This denies Scotus's proposal of a *haecceitas* formally distinct from matter and form in the individual.
3. It is impossible for contradictories to be simultaneously true about one and the same being. This denies the ascription of both universality and non-universality to an individual being.

Ockham's conclusion is that universals occur only in the understanding and not in any extra-mental things; they are nothing but conventional names for observable similarities.

While Ockham is usually regarded as a nominalist, the "conceptualist" label is sometimes used as well. "Terminism" is perhaps best, for it keeps us from too readily identifying him with either Roscelin's earlier nominalism or Abelard's conceptualism. For Roscelin only words have universal reference, and nothing else. Abelard spoke of the universal in relation to a logical *content,* whereas Ockham speaks of it in relation to a mental *act.* Abelard allows exemplars of genera and species in God's

---

7. For a full and clear account of Ockham's arguments and positions, see Marilyn McCord Adams, *William Ockham* (Univ. of Notre Dame Press, 1987), 2 vols.

mind, while Ockham does not. Moreover, the earlier debate focused on either metaphysical problems about the ordered nature of things, or psychological problems about the abstraction of forms from particulars, whereas Ockham focuses on the logical problem of how general terms can stand indiscriminately for a number of individuals.

Initially, he regarded the universal as a thought-object, a kind of generalized mental picture we form of similar things we have experienced.

> And this can be called a universal, because it is a pattern and relates indifferently to all the singular things outside the mind. . . . And in this way a universal is not the result of generation [innate], but of abstraction, which is only a kind of mental picturing.[8]

But this view implied that we as well as God know things indirectly through the concept, rather than knowing them directly. Ockham thus came to think of the universal as a particular *act* of knowing that signifies many particulars.

> The mind's own intellectual acts are called states of mind. By their nature they stand for the actual things outside the mind or for other things in the mind, just as spoken words stand for them by convention. By such a common or confused intellection, singular things outside the mind are known. For instance, to say that we have a confused intellection of man, means that we have a cognition by which we do not understand one man rather than another, but that . . . we have cognition of a man rather than a donkey. In consequence . . . an infinity of objects can be known by such a confused cognition.[9]

This mental act, then, is not a mental representation of a property common to all the species, nor is it a universal concept abstracted from the actual species; it is rather an act of referring in a general manner to what we directly perceive.

This view of general terms requires very little metaphysical apparatus, for all that exists is particular acts and particular substances

8. William of Ockham, *Philosophical Writings*, trans. P. Boehner (Bobbs-Merrill, 1964), p. 44.
9. Boehner, *Philosophical Writings*, pp. 47-48.

with particular qualities we can be directly aware of. It reflects the principle of parsimony known as Ockham's razor: that we should never multiply entities more than is necessary — that is to say, unless they are required by reason or experience or some infallible authority.[10]

The consequences of "terminism" were quite apparent, and Ockham embraced them readily. A contingent creation without inherent logical necessities can only be known by direct perception of existent objects. We can think "abstractly" of similar particulars without knowing of their existence, but this is very different from the abstraction of universal principles from particulars in Aristotelian epistemology, and from abstract general ideas in Abelard's conceptualism. Ockham opens the way to the purely empirical approach of Baconian science.[11]

Without eternal forms known by the human soul, arguments based on them — which since the time of Plato had supposedly proved the existence and immortality of the soul — are now impossible. Immortality must be accepted purely by faith. Without inherent essences of an Aristotelian sort, we can know nothing of final causes. For Ockham, all talk of nature acting unconsciously for an end is pure metaphor. Without formal and final causes then, only material and efficient causes remain, and causal explanations of a mechanist sort alone are possible. The teleological worldviews of Aristotle and Aquinas are therefore out, and the door is open to the mechanistic science of the Renaissance. The nominalist movement became the wedge driven between theology and philosophy; and the scholastic synthesis was essentially broken. Theology was left without philosophical bases and explanations, apart from the probabilistic causal arguments of the empiricist.

Likewise with ethics. The moral order, like everything else in creation, is contingent rather than necessary. It is implicit in theism that our moral obligation is to God and what he commands, and that the ontological ground of the moral order lies in the Creator/creature relationship. Augustine, Aquinas, Scotus, and Ockham all agree on this. But Ockham, like Scotus, grounds morality in God's sovereign will,

10. Adams, *William Ockham*, p. 156.

11. Michael Foster has argued in a series of articles, "The Christian Doctrine of Creation and the Rise of Modern Natural Science" (*Mind* 43 [1934]: 446; 44 [1935]: 439; 45 [1936]: 1), that emphasis on the contingency of creation underlay the rise of empirical methods in science. With no intrinsic necessity that nature be this way or that, we have to look and see for ourselves.

rather than in his intellect with its unchanging universal exemplars. Beyond what divine revelation declares, we can therefore have no certain knowledge. Even the present moral order is questionable, for God could logically sanction anything other than a logical contradiction. The tendency against fixed moral rules is stronger even than in Duns Scotus.

Several matters stand out. First, according to Ockham our highest obligation is still the obligation to God — still, in Ockham's thought, our highest good. While we cannot prove this to be logically necessary without assuming God's existence, if only one God exists then it follows that he is to be loved above all else. He must be loved for himself, as we would love a friend, and not just out of self-interested desire. This self-forgetting love for God is the one act that cannot possibly be evil; other obligations are secondary since they depend on particular divine precepts remaining in force. Not so love for God. He could allow polygamy in the Old Testament and order Abraham to kill Isaac; such acts, performed out of love for God, would be virtuous, although they would not be as long as the present laws of God remain in force. But could God not command that he be hated? The command may be possible, but not its fulfillment, for true obedience to any divine command is itself an act of love for God. To hate God out of love for God would be an impossible, self-contradictory thing. God might *cause* someone to hate him, and so be a partial cause of that hatred, but to hate him out of love for him is not possible.[12]

Second, Ockham is a voluntarist; the primary locus of moral right and of virtue is the human will. It is not *what* one does but *why* one does it that has merit.

> the act primarily and principally virtuous is the act of will. This is obvious because that alone is primarily praiseworthy and blameworthy. But others are so only secondarily . . . through the fact that they are elicited in conformity with an act of will.[13]

12. See Lucan Freppert, *The Bases of Morality According to William Ockham* (Franciscan Herald Press, 1988), ch. 4, esp. p. 135, *passim;* Boehner, *Philosophical Writings,* pp. 160-63.

13. Ockham's *Commentary on the Sentences,* bk. 3, q. 12, excerpted in A. Hyman and J. Walsh, *Philosophy in the Middle Ages* (Hackett, 1973), p. 646. Cp. Boehner, *Philosophical Writings,* pp. 160-63; Gordon Leff, *William of Ockham: The Metamorphosis of Scholastic Discourse* (Rowman & Littlefield, 1975), pp. 476-526; and Freppert, *The Bases of Morality,* ch. 3.

Soft determinist

Acts can also be done for a bad end and with bad intention; they can be performed out of compulsion or impulse, even caused by God. He knows and concurs in each act of the human will, and without his cooperation no creature could act at all. God is a necessary though partial cause of every act of will, but he cannot wholly cause a free act. No act is meritorious unless it is voluntary. Nor is it meritorious simply to will what God wills. (He willed Judas's betrayal and Jesus' death.) We must will what God would will, and do so because he wills that we will it out of love for him.[14]

Third, how can we know what God wills us to will? Some of the ten commandments are contingent decrees that God might hypothetically change. And where there is no divine revelation to command us, how should we choose? God wills right reason or conscience to be the norm. We may be mistaken as to what these require, for neither conscience nor reason is infallible; but they provide a prudential and discernible code. The right to property, for example, is a remedy for the greed and violence that have marred humanity since the fall, and so accords with right reason. God could have ordered things differently; in special circumstances he could exclude us from the right to property because of the consequences, and in an ideal order there might be no such right at all. While such rights are logically prior to any human convention about them, they still depend on God's will that we follow right reason.[15]

Ockham speaks of natural right in three ways. First, there are norms conforming to natural reason, such as prohibitions on lying and adultery. Only God could change these. Second, some norms may be modified by positive laws we enact, such as those regarding common ownership of property and the extent of individual liberty. Third, some may be inferred from the *ius gentium* we find in human behavior, like the fact that violence may be repelled by force. All these are matters of natural right for the present order and are known by right reason, but they are ultimately grounded in what the author and ruler of nature prohibits or commands.[16]

14. Freppert, *The Bases of Morality,* p. 120.

15. Copleston, *History of Philosophy,* vol. 3, p. 115.

16. Ockham's *Dialogues on Imperial and Papal Power,* referred to in N. Kretzman, A. Kenny, and Jan Pinborg, eds., *The Cambridge History of Later Medieval Philosophy* (Cambridge Univ. Press, 1982), p. 714.

con-
sequences

The outcome of all this is the rejection of a metaphysically grounded natural law ethic and of the idea of a moral universe. The intrinsic union of fact and value is no longer accepted. Instead, we rely on God-given reason to prudently order our present world. The theist may well find this initially acceptable. But when the underlying theology gets discarded and replaced by mechanistic empirical science, then a relativistic and consequentialist ethics is likely to prevail.

Meanwhile, Protestant Reformers felt the force of the Ockhamist trend. Martin Luther studied under nominalist teachers at Erfurt and at one point called Ockham "my dear master."[17] His education involved a close study of Aristotle's *Ethics* and *Metaphysics,* and he knew well both the philosophy and the theology of late medieval nominalists. Yet he found the study of philosophy hard, and when assigned to teach Aristotle's *Ethics* he commented that he would rather exchange it for theology.[18] Aristotle, he complained, had conquered the schools and usurped the authority of Christ and the Scriptures. Instead of Scripture giving light to reason, Aristotle was now used to give light to Scripture. In an address in 1520 to the German nobility he even proposes discarding Aristotle from the university curriculum, apart from the *Organon, Rhetoric,* and *Poetics.* Ockham may have tried to restore what he thought to be a true understanding of Aristotle, but Luther thought they all misunderstood him, since in actuality Aristotle confined himself to nature without going into theological questions at all.[19]

Luther's particular objection to Aristotle was the nominalist one he doubtless learned at Erfurt. He quips that in philosophy "substantia" refers to essence, the inner nature of a thing, its form, while in Scripture to have "substance" is to have riches that last. Luther was concerned not with inner essences, but with the external conditions of human life and the quality of relationships.[20]

17. B. A. Gerrish, "Luther," in *Encyclopedia of Philosophy* (Macmillan, 1967), vol. 5, p. 112.

18. Gerhard Ebeling, *Luther: An Introduction to His Thought* (Fortress, 1964), ch. 5.

19. B. A. Gerrish, *Grace and Reason: A Study in the Theology of Luther* (Clarendon, 1962), p. 36. Luther's colleague Melanchthon meanwhile retained an Aristotelian viewpoint, while being hostile to Scholasticism as such.

20. Ebeling, *Luther: An Introduction,* p. 88. Cp. Gerrish, *Grace and Reason,* ch. 3.

It would have been better for the church if Porphyry with his universals had not been born for the use of theologians.[21]

On the role of reason likewise, he followed the Ockhamists. Rejecting real universals, they rejected the first principles Aristotle and Aquinas required as universal premises for ethical reasoning. The Franciscans generally, including Bonaventure and Ockham, were in any case wary of syllogistic proofs and preferred a dialectic that criticizes all knowledge claims. This became the new logic of the *via moderna*, and Luther preferred it. "Nothing is so closely reasoned that it cannot be contradicted by reasoning," he says.[22] In the Bible, purely human knowledge is carnal and fails to understand spiritual things; the true knowledge is of God in Christ, and this comes by faith.

> In temporal things and human relations, man is rational enough; there he needs no other light than reason. So God does not teach us in Scripture how to milk cows, build houses, and know that 100 guilders are more than 10. But in divine things, our nature is stone blind.[23]

There is a tension here about reason. On the one hand, Luther declared that whereas by human reason 2 + 5 = 7, yet, if God should declare them 8, one must believe contrary to reason and to feeling.[24] On the other hand, reason can build and rule cities, and he prizes liberal learning.

> You parents cannot prepare a more dependable treasure for your children than an education in the liberal arts. House and home burn down and disappear, but an education is easy to carry off.[25]

While he warns about the falsehoods of philosophers and sophists, he speaks positively of history, music, classical languages, poetry, and mathematics, and wants the income of monasteries to be used for maintaining schools and universities.

---

21. Luther's 1517 *Disputation Against Scholastic Theology*, sec. 52, in *Luther's Works*, vol. 31 (Muhlenberg Press, 1957).

22. *What Luther Says*, compiled by E. M. Plass (Concordia, 1959), p. 1160.

23. *What Luther Says*, p. 1158.

24. Roland Bainton, *Here I Stand: A Life of Martin Luther* (Mentor, 1950), pp. 169-70.

25. *What Luther Says*, p. 446.

The nominalists, by their criticism of realist views of universals, had torn the scholastic synthesis of faith and reason apart. For Luther, the basic problem is reason's usurpation of biblical authority, and even Ockham did not fully escape that snare. Ockham's voluntarism presented far too optimistic an account of human freedom, implying that we can by nature choose to love God and so prepare ourselves to receive God's grace. With some of his followers he had even been accused of Pelagianism. Luther spots the intrusion of reason where it does not belong. Love of God supposedly prepares one for salvation; loving God is a virtue, a virtue is an inner habit, and in Aristotle such habits are formed by repeated choices under the rule of reason. But reason has nothing at all to do with salvation or with our preparation for it. If this intrusion of reason into the gospel results from the *via moderna*, then Luther will fight the *via moderna*.

According to Gerrish, Luther developed his understanding of justification by faith in response to voluntarism. Ockham thought of grace as a quality of soul infused by God to aid the will in loving God meritoriously, and based this on the freedom of will he ascribed to both humankind and God. Luther sees grace simply as God's goodwill forgiving us, and bases this on the atoning work of Christ. So he attacks Ockham's voluntarism.

In a series of theses he proposed for a student at Wittenberg to defend, he asserts the following:

5. It is false to state that man's inclination is free to choose between two opposites. Indeed, the inclination is not free, but captive.
6. It is false to state that will can by nature conform to correct precepts. This is said in opposition to Scotus and to Gabriel [Biel, an influential nominalist].[26]
7. As a matter of fact, without the grace of God the will produces an act that is perverse and evil.
17. Man is by nature unable to want God to be God. Indeed, he himself wants to be God, and does not want God to be God.
41. Virtually the entire *Ethics* of Aristotle is the worst enemy of grace.
43. It is an error to say that no man can become a theologian without

26. See H. A. Oberman, *The Harvest of Medieval Theology: Gabriel Biel and Late Medieval Nominalism* (Harvard Univ. Press, 1963).

Aristotle. Indeed, no one can become a theologian unless he becomes one without Aristotle.[27]

All of this — Luther's relation to the Ockhamist view of reason, to nominalism, and to voluntarism — underlies his ethic. Reason cannot decide what is right and wrong before God and does not know the way to God. It knows that God is, but not who and what God is — a far cry from Augustine and Aquinas on God being demonstrably the Good. Commenting on Isaiah 60:1-6 ("Arise, shine; for your light has come . . . and nations shall come to your light"), he says that the prophet rejects the natural light of reason as an intermediary stage between darkness and the light of the gospel.[28]

On the other hand, we can judge in the human and worldly matters referred to in the second table of the decalogue, because in creating us God inscribed those laws in human reason. Luther takes the statement of the apostle Paul about the Gentiles showing the law written on their hearts to be about natural right, and the inner intention of this natural law is nothing else than the biblical law of love.[29]

Luther's ethic, then, closely follows Ockham's except in its view of free will and of grace. The Ockhamist Gabriel Biel, less than fifty years before Luther, wrote that natural law becomes little more than right reason based on human experience.[30] Luther essentially agrees. Since nature affords the experience on which natural reason reflects, the substance of natural law is neither innate in the human mind nor intrinsic to an unchanging natural order. Metaphysics contributes nothing to ethics; revelation and right reason alone do.

John Calvin also was exposed to nominalism in the course of his education in Paris. He too studied Ockhamist writers, but this influence was greatly moderated by that of the Stoics, who were then in vogue as a counterbalance to Epicurean tendencies in the Italian Renaissance. While some Renaissance Christian humanists turned to Plato, others gravitated to the Stoics as their patristic predecessors had done, this

---

27. *Disputation Against Scholastic Theology.* This issue is the main focus of Gerrish's book, and explains its title, *Grace and Reason.*

28. Gerrish, *Grace and Reason,* pp. 12-14.

29. See Paul Althaus, *The Ethics of Martin Luther,* trans. R. C. Schultz (Fortress, 1972), ch. 2.

30. Oberman, *The Harvest of Medieval Theology,* ch. 4.

time because of the value the Stoics placed on human beings as such, because of their love of knowledge and truth, and because their ethic of natural law provided a basis for just government and social harmony. Erasmus eulogized Seneca, and Calvin wrote a commentary on Seneca's *De Clementia* in which he traced resemblances between Christianity and Stoicism, while still complaining of the Stoics' inability to come to reliable conclusions and their indifference to human need.[31]

Stoic natural law theory had been adopted by the Roman Cicero in response to the ethical skeptics of his day, and transmitted thereby to Roman jurisprudence and Christian thought. Augustine himself draws on it. Wrote Cicero:

> True law is right reason in agreement with nature; it is of universal application, unchanging and everlasting. . . . It is a sin to try to alter this law, nor is it allowable to attempt to repeal any part of it, and it is impossible to abolish it entirely. . . . There will be one master and one ruler, that is, God, over us all, for He is the author of this law, its promulgator, and its enforcing judge.[32]

Nature and right reason command us. Right reason means understanding the causes and consequences of human actions in a law-governed (logos-governed) universe. Right reason thereby agrees with nature *(jus naturale)*, and is universally apparent in the laws that are common to all nations *(jus gentium)*, rather than in positive laws enacted in the interests of an individual ruler or particular state.

This Stoic influence moderates Calvin's position. First, while he too stresses the complete sovereignty of the divine will, he is careful to guard against "the notion of the Roman theologians concerning the absolute and arbitrary power of God" — a reference perhaps to extreme nominalists who read Ockham that way. God, Calvin goes on, is not lawless, "who is a law to himself."[33] Calvin believed in a rational God and a rationally ordered creation, echoing Stoicism's rational providence in a logos-structured universe.

---

31. See Francois Wendel, *Calvin: The Origins and Development of His Religious Thought*, trans. P. Mairet (Harper & Row, 1950), ch. 1. See also Q. Breen, *John Calvin: A Study of French Humanism* (Archon Books, 1968), ch. 4.

32. Cicero, *De Re Publica*, III.xxii.33. Cp. *De Officiis*, I.4; III.5.

33. John Calvin, *Institutes of the Christian Religion* (8th American ed.; Eerdmans, 1949), III.23.2.

Second, the image of God that distinguishes humans from other animals is human reason. This image

> denotes the integrity which Adam possessed, when he was endowed with a right understanding, when he had affection, regulated by reason, and all his senses governed in proper order, and when, in the excellency of his nature, he truly resembled the excellence of his Creator.[34]

Human understanding can "discriminate between objects, as they shall respectively appear deserving of approbation and disapprobation of the will," so that we "choose and follow what the understanding shall have pronounced to be good."[35]

Nor is human reason destroyed by the fall, as some of Calvin's critics mistakenly claim.

> Reason, by which man distinguishes between good and evil, by which he understands and judges, being a natural talent, could not be totally destroyed, but is partly debilitated, partly vitiated . . . some sparks continue to shine in the nature of man, even in its corrupt and degenerate state, that prove him to be a rational creature. . . .[36]

Third, we know how we ought to live because we are "sufficiently instructed by that natural law of which the Apostle speaks."[37] The conscience is sufficiently discerning to deprive us of any excuse of ignorance. Like Scotus, Ockham, and Luther, Calvin sees the decalogue as a re-publication of natural law, and he too distinguishes two tables of the law. Natural reason falls far short of reaching the principal points of the first, in that they concern our relationship to God; but it is "a little clearer" about the second table, which addresses the preservation of civil society. He quotes Cicero to the effect that natural laws are the "souls of states," yet no state is well constituted, Calvin claims, that "neglects the policy of Moses and is governed by the common laws of nations."[38] For the law of God that we call moral law

34. *Inst.*, I.15.3.
35. *Inst.*, I.15.7.
36. *Inst.*, II.2.12.
37. *Inst.*, II.2.22.
38. *Inst.*, IV.20.14.

is no other than a declaration of natural law, and of that conscience which has been engraven of God on the minds of men. . . .[39]

Calvin makes no reference to either fixed essences or an immanent teleology that provides natural ends as the good we should pursue, for he follows the Stoics in a more conceptualist than realist direction. This is a rationally ordered universe by virtue of divine creation and providence, not by means of unchanging forms; and we know natural law by exercising natural reason's God-given powers of discernment. There is no immanent metaphysical basis for values, or for regarding the universe as intrinsically moral. It is moral only contingently, for any moral order is upheld by the enforcement of moral law through God's providential governance.

The natural law therefore has the authority of God-given right reason, not a God-given inner telos. Our inner tendency since the fall is asocial, a fearful and dangerous state that only God's grace can reform. Natural law must therefore be enforced by proper governmental power; but this calls for a broader political participation than the medievals and Reformers had known. And broader political participation created its own problems for ethics.

39. *Inst.,* IV.20.16.

CHAPTER EIGHT

Right Reason and the Scientific Revolution

THE OCKHAMIST REACTION was by no means a passing phenomenon at the end of Scholastic philosophy. It continued to be a powerful force in early modern thought and still continues today. Ockham was eagerly embraced in fourteenth-century Oxford. In fact, his teaching produced such a flood of acceptance that in 1322 the Chancellor was dismissed for opposing "modern ideas," and the intellectual rivalry with Aristotelianism continued well into the fifteenth century.[1] Although Aristotle was still taught, the decline of traditional forms of thought encouraged the separation of Aristotelian logic from metaphysics and of philosophical reasoning from theology. The public burning of Scotus's texts at Oxford in 1550 signaled a total repudiation of Scholastic philosophy, and by the time Francis Bacon arrived at Cambridge around 1557, the new methods had there too replaced the old.

As a result of this change, Paoli Rossi affirms:

> the typical seventeenth-century intellectual probings are a direct legacy of Ockhamist empiricism, the Ockhamist concept of knowledge as experience, and of nominalism. . . . A new science of nature

---

1. See M. H. Carré, *Phases of Thought in England* (Clarendon, 1949), ch. 5.

and a new form of religious belief were inspired by Ockham's notion of experience.[2]

But his was not the only influence at work. The Protestant Reformation affected the intellectual climate in general, and such individuals as Bacon and Hobbes in particular. The Reformation coincided, through the recovery of the writings of Sextus Empiricus, with a resurgence of arguments drawn from Greek skepticism that later became evident in the work of Montaigne, Gassendi, and Mersenne. The famous controversy between Erasmus and Luther had focused on whether there are rational grounds for belief when the final authority of the church is rejected in favor of Scripture alone: if the priesthood of all believers places the onus on individual conscience, does not the specter of sectarian anarchy appear? Erasmus resolved this problem by advocating acceptance of the church's decrees, while Luther found subjective certainty in a faith convinced solely by Scripture. "Here I stand. I can do no other," he affirmed. Calvin likewise took Scripture as the only final rule of faith, subjecting the mind to the witness of the Holy Spirit. With the post-Reformation breakdown of church authority, a quest for certainty became the dominant epistemological issue in both theology and philosophy.[3]

Into this vacuum of authority came the new science. The mechanistic explanation of nature in terms of matter and motion was a conscious reversion to Democritus's atomism. With no substantial forms and no inherent teleology, matter becomes nothing but spatially extended stuff devoid of all other qualities and potentials. In itself it has none of the capacity Aquinas saw in it for order, change, beauty, or the good; it lacks all secondary qualities, being colorless, silent, passive, and dead. Natural forces are likewise blind, not end-oriented at all except in the hands of some external agent. The contrast with the Scholastic vision of nature as good, imitating the Divine Goodness, could hardly be stronger. There is found in nature itself no evidence of the purposiveness of causal processes, no explanation of the ordered

2. Paoli Rossi, *Francis Bacon,* trans. S. Rabinovitch (Univ. of Chicago Press, 1968), p. x.

3. See R. H. Popkin, *The History of Skepticism from Erasmus to Descartes* (Harper Torchbooks, 1968), ch. 1; Stephen Toulmin, *Cosmopolis* (Free Press, 1990), chs. 1-2; J. Stout, *The Flight from Authority* (Univ. of Notre Dame Press, 1981).

individuality of persons, and no basis for values of any sort. Nature is impersonal and value-free, a concatenation of material atoms in motion.

The Ockhamist rejection of Aristotelian metaphysics undoubtedly led to the rise of this new science. So did the Reformation emphasis on divine sovereignty. Because natural laws are contingent, not necessary, God could have imposed a different set of laws. Luther pointed out that, as we cannot become righteous by our own efforts, so nature cannot change by its own efforts. Says Calvin,

> For we do not, with the Stoics, imagine a necessity arising from a perpetual concatenation and intricate series of causes, contained in nature, but we make God the Arbiter and Governor of all things, who . . . by his own power, executes what he has decreed. Whence we assert that [all things] are so governed by his providence, as to be directed to the end appointed by it.[4]

Calvinist Occasionalists took this to deny all natural causes, even the existence of matter. God's providence, like the original creation, is *ex nihilo*. But more moderate positions settled for inert matter governed by laws ordained by God's providence.

These three influences — nominalism, the Reformation, and the new science — converged in seventeenth-century philosophy, so that attempts to ground ethics were inevitably tied to new epistemological and metaphysical approaches. In effect, two directions emerge, one reminiscent of Stoicism — that is, a law-governed order without the inherent teleology of Aristotle and the Scholastics — and one that emphasizes God's commands and develops the empirical approach implicit in nominalism.

The philosophies of Descartes and Spinoza represent the first of these directions. Descartes's procedure in his *Meditations* recognizes the impact of skepticism, and the reasons he gives for doubting are characteristic of Pyrrhonism: the equipollence of arguments and the relativity of perception. But he offers a new method for overcoming doubt, one modeled on the mathematical reasoning that characterized much of

---

4. *Institutes of the Christian Religion*, I.16.8. See also Gary Deason, "Reformation Theology and the Mechanistic Conception of Nature," in *God and Nature*, ed. D. C. Lindberg and R. L. Numbers (Univ. of California Press, 1986), pp. 167-91; and E. Gilson, *From Aristotle to Darwin and Back Again*, trans. John Lyon (Univ. of Notre Dame Press, 1984), ch. 2.

continental European science, namely, deductive proofs from axiomatic first truths that are themselves guaranteed by the fact that the light of reason is God-given. Crucial to this move is his treatment of error in *Meditation IV*, where, asserting the integrity of both will and intellect, he requires that we withhold judgment rather than risk error whenever we lack clear and distinct ideas. The assumption is that the will is entirely free and fully self-controlled, rather than drawn by some inner teleology in a proper direction. It is as if the will operates in a causal vacuum, where neither efficient nor final causes affect it. As Copleston points out,[5] free will is for Descartes a primary datum, logically prior to *cogito ergo sum*. I can even choose to doubt my bodily existence.

Descartes in fact rejects the Scholastic doctrine of real forms or natures, and ignores the Logos doctrine to which Christian thinkers throughout the Middle Ages had appealed. He is a conceptualist, valuing knowledge for its usefulness to humans rather than as part of a teleology that draws us towards the good. While he offers no systematic ethical theory, his account of the passions suggests an essentially Stoic position. It is a causal account of impulses and desires, rather than of natural ends in a teleologically ordered world. Freedom of will guided by right reason enables us to master our passions, so that life may be more bearable and we can enjoy the contentment of soul that such virtue brings. Human perfection is to have the power of acting freely to change what we can, and to have an untroubled mind about things we cannot change.

In his *Discourse on Method* he adopts a provisional morality to guide his actions while rebuilding his philosophy. He will obey the laws and customs of his country and adhere to his religion, but where opinions differ he will choose the more moderate ones, lest he stray too far into error. He will be firm and resolute in following even the most dubious opinions he holds, lest he suffer the anxieties of wandering aimlessly through life. He intends to conquer himself rather than fortune, changing his desires rather than the world, because nothing is entirely within our control except our thoughts. Finally, he opts for the philosophical life because its satisfactions free him from concern about things he cannot change. It is a prudential ethic, echoing the Stoic concern for *apathia*, freedom from pain in the body and trouble in the soul.[6]

5. F. Copleston, *A History of Philosophy* (St. Martin's Press, 1950), vol. 4, ch. 6.
6. See Charles Taylor, *Sources of The Self* (Harvard Univ. Press, 1989), ch. 8.

The Cartesian ethic is implicit in his famous mind/body dualism. Intellect and will are functions of an immaterial mind, a substance separate from the body with its causal processes. As mind rules body, so reason stands outside of nature and can sometimes bend it to our will. Mind was previously seen as part of nature, ruled by God-given natural law for God-given natural ends; now mind is free. The metaphysically grounded ethic of the past is thus transformed into a scientifically oriented one, with temporal benefits. Science in effect assumes the authority, previously held by the divine Logos, over both human thought and human life.

Benedict Spinoza was profoundly influenced by Descartes's method and produced a similar kind of ethic, but his nature-pantheism provides a metaphysic closer to the Stoics. The Stoics spoke of nature's law-governed order as itself the divine Logos, and carried this over into their view of the human self. Mind and body are not separate substances, but two aspects of one material being. For Spinoza, likewise, all being, whether the infinite whole or its finite modes, manifests two attributes: thought and spatial extension. Consequently, emotions are physically caused drives accompanied by confused ideas, and they can hold us in bondage unless they are changed or dispelled by adequate clarity of mind. Freedom lies not in uncaused choices or actions (nothing is uncaused), but in the rational acceptance of a causal order we cannot change. We may not be able to alter our external circumstances, but clear and distinct ideas about the causal order and its effects on us will dispel adverse emotions. Virtue consists, therefore, in a life ruled not by fear but by rational, scientific knowledge. The Stoic ethic prevails.

On the other hand, the nominalist influence in seventeenth-century ethics is evident in Francis Bacon and Thomas Hobbes, for English science at the time was generally more empirical than on the continent. Bacon had studied Aristotle and Greek science at Cambridge, but like many others of his time found much of it uninspiring and sterile. The Scholastic controversies surrounding Scotus in particular were unrelated to the realities of this life, and the Scholastic method itself seemed a kind of idle sophistry. Natural theology was powerless; believers did not need it, and unbelievers were unconvinced by it. Syllogistic reasoning lets nature slip out of its hands: the words making up its propositions are but tokens of concepts. If our concepts are improperly and too hastily abstracted from facts, then the whole edifice collapses. In 2,000 years, moreover, Aristotelianism had failed to restore humanity's dominion over creation, and Bacon was filled with disgust at so much misguided effort. Among the philosophical positions he repudiates as "Idols of the Theatre" is that of Aristotle,

> who corrupted natural philosophy by his logic, fashioning the world out of categories. . . .[7]

The criticism of "abstracting" concepts from facts reaches beyond Aristotle's epistemology to the theory of forms and the whole teleological view of nature.

> The final cause rather corrupts than advances the sciences, except such as have to do with human action. The discovery of the formal is despaired of.[8]

Even efficient and material causes contribute little without reference to particular processes, for nothing exists in nature besides particular bodies functioning according to fixed causal laws. These laws are the only forms that interest Bacon. He therefore confines himself to investigating material and efficient causes alone, and leaves questions of purpose to theology.

In making this move, he consciously favors Democritus's atomism because it anticipated the new mechanistic science. He realizes this means that the hierarchical order of nature must go, but earthly things will thereby assume higher priority. In addition, the intrinsic connection of scientific with religious understanding gives way to an incidental and external one in which science may be made to serve God's purposes without itself telling us what those purposes are. Such a separation was prudent in a day when theological divisions and religious persecution were omnipresent; Galileo's case alone advised keeping science independent of religious authority.

Ockham's influence may be seen not only in Bacon's exclusion of formal and final causes, but also in his empirical methods. Galileo

---

7. F. Bacon, *Novum Organum,* Aphorism 63. See also the preface to his *Great Instauration;* also Paoli Rossi, *Francis Bacon,* p. 40, *passim;* F. H. Anderson, *The Philosophy of Francis Bacon* (Univ. of Chicago Press, 1948), ch. 12; Anthony Quinton, *Francis Bacon* (Hill & Wang, 1980), ch. 4.

8. Aphorism II.

himself was influenced by the nominalist view of causation that replaced the search for essences with the study of the actual behavior of things. A. C. Crombie points to Ockham's claim that we directly perceive particulars, and to his interest in tracing recurrences of the same effect produced by different causes, as a clear anticipation of later inductive procedures.[9] Bacon's method was through and through empirical, tabulating observations, noting variables, and finding uniformities. While he gave no place to mathematical methods or to the role of hypotheses, he was convinced that we could achieve a highly reliable and vastly expanded knowledge of nature. And in contrast to the contemplation of unchanging forms, he was interested in *causing* change. Envisioning the scientific utopia that knowledge could produce, his optimism was almost unbounded. Perhaps more than any of his contemporaries, Bacon saw that knowledge of nature's ways was a form of power.

But Bacon was also a politician and courtier, and he knew about the abuses of power and the need for ethical guidance. While no natural moral law can be derived from science, religion provides a moral direction. It is religion rather than natural law that gives purpose and value to science. Bacon's mother was a devout Calvinist; he himself used prayers that reflect Reformation influences, and his concern for earthly affairs and ordinary aspects of life was characteristic of Reformed religion.[10] He thus derives the purpose of science from the biblical understanding of humans as stewards of God's creation.

> For man, by the fall, lost at once his state of innocence and his empire over creation, both of which can be partially recovered even in this life, the first by religion and faith, the second by the arts and sciences.[11]

Since the power of knowledge can be misused, Bacon distinguishes three kinds of ambition:

---

9. A. C. Crombie, *Augustine to Galileo: The History of Science, A.D. 400-1650* (Harvard Univ. Press, 1953), p. 231. Cp. T. D. Bozeman, *Protestants in an Age of Science* (Univ. of North Carolina Press, 1977), p. 5, *passim.*

10. See Charles Taylor, *Sources of the Self,* ch. 13.

11. *Novum Organum,* Aphorism II.52. See B. Farrington, *Francis Bacon: Philosopher of Industrial Science* (Collier Books, 1961).

First, that of men who are anxious to enlarge their own power in their country, which is a vulgar and degenerate kind; next, that of men who strive to enlarge the power and empire of their country over mankind, which is more dignified but not less covetous; but if one were to endeavor to renew and enlarge the power and empire of mankind in general over the universe, such ambition is both more sound and more noble than the other two.[12]

Power, he says, must be governed by "right reason" and true religion. This is the same moral prescription that Ockham had given — divine commands plus right reason judging what is prudent in relieving and improving the human condition. It is a utilitarian ethic with religious justification; it reflects a more biblical than Greek view of knowledge in that knowing and doing are connected in serving the kingdom of God. Bacon sees human knowledge as the means to a scientific utopia that will be the kingdom of God on earth.

His ethic is teleological, but his view of nature is not. The good is what God purposes, without an immanent teleology in nature. No philosophy, he contends, can by itself determine the final good, for the rational soul is made in the image of God, not of nature. Because of our desire for self-preservation, the light and laws of nature teach us what is prudent, and self knowledge leads to cultivating the mind. Natural knowledge of virtue and vice is thus possible by right reason, but no clear vision of the final good; nor can reason prescribe a cure for our moral failings. In this, we need both the law and the grace of God.[13]

Bacon's separation of science from theology distances knowledge of nature from knowledge of God, and so from knowledge of the good. In denying that nature imitates divine goodness he concludes that humans alone bear any image or likeness of God. We find ourselves, then, in a morally indifferent world, no longer the moral universe it was once believed to be.

It falls to Thomas Hobbes to draw out the consequences of this revolution more fully. Hobbes was by no means a disinterested theorizer.

12. Aphorism I.129. Peter Schouls finds a similar quest for scientific mastery over nature in Descartes. See his *Descartes and the Enlightenment* (McGill-Queen's Univ. Press, 1989).

13. This line of thought is developed by F. H. Anderson, *Francis Bacon,* pp. 171-73.

Born in Elizabethan England at the time of the Spanish Armada, coming to manhood amid growing conflicts between king and parliament, he was well acquainted with sectarian rivalry, religious persecution, and the political conflicts that erupted into civil war. He himself was ousted by clerics from his position as mathematics tutor for Prince Charles, later to become Charles II, and because of conspiracies against himself he fled from exile in France back to Cromwell's England.[14] He feared two main threats to peace and safety: Catholicism's domination of the state, and the priesthood of all believers, with its attendant sectarian rivalry. His attitude to such "private judgment" is plain.

> What bloodshed hath not this erroneous doctrine caused, that kings are not superiors to, but administrators for the multitude? Lastly, how many rebellions hath this opinion been the cause of, which teacheth that the knowledge whether the commands of kings be just or unjust belongs to private men, and that before they yield obedience, they not only may, but ought to dispute them.[15]

On church and state, therefore, Hobbes found the Erastian position best, by which the state legislates those details of religious doctrine and practice over which individuals and sects tend to fight. This, he was convinced, is the safest policy.[16]

As for the political conflict, Hobbes had royalist sympathies. He was very much the Renaissance humanist, educated in the classics, a translator of Thucydides, enamored of such aristocratic values as beauty, honor, magnanimity, and courage; he lavished praise on the heroic virtues of the Cavendish family with whom he lived for many years.[17] But he rejected both the divine right of kings and the Scholastic doctrine of natural law on prudential and philosophical grounds. On the one hand, divine right is itself a matter of dispute and therefore no solution to sectarian conflict. On the other hand, Hobbes had studied Aristotle and the Scholastics at Oxford and had grown increasingly dissatisfied

---

14. See Sterling Lamprecht, introduction to *De Cive* (Appleton-Century-Crofts, 1949).

15. Lamprecht, introduction to *De Cive,* p. 9.

16. Hobbes, *Leviathan,* xxvi, xlii. Cp. Richard Peters, *Hobbes* (Greenwood, 1956), ch. 10.

17. Leo Strauss, *The Political Philosophy of Hobbes* (Univ. of Chicago Press, 1952), ch. 3.

with them. Having worked as Bacon's private secretary, he doubtless knew that Richard Hooker's view of natural law was too close to Aquinas for Bacon's liking.[18] Hobbes, too, adopts a nominalist position. It was Aristotle who gave religion the erroneous doctrine that essences are substantial forms, whereas in fact they are simply words that distinguish *what* something is from the simple fact *that* it is.[19] But if there are no real essences, there can be no natural law ethic or political theory of the Scholastic sort. Where then do we turn?

Hobbes's solution to this pressing practical question (and to the vacuum of authority) in seventeenth-century political and religious life was that we must place government on a scientific rather than a theological basis. He was nearly fifty before the methods of Galileo and Descartes awakened him to the possibilities of such a change, and it was a kind of philosophical conversion. If "the end of knowledge is power,"[20] he could avoid both subservience to the church and sectarian conflicts by making politics into a science. He hoped his tombstone would indicate that he was the discoverer of the science of "natural justice."

The science he has in mind follows the method Galileo used in physics, of resolving a matter under investigation into its constitutive causes and examining them singly, then recomposing them into a whole in a way that explains the overall behavior.[21] The immediate outcome is Hobbes's strong individualism. He begins his initial work, *De Cive,* by describing the behavior of the individuals who make up society. His own experience of human nature is evident in what he describes. It is a strongly individualistic account, explicitly denying the traditional assumption that we are by nature social beings, born fit for society. On the contrary, we are governed not by reason but by self-interested passion. We come together by accident, out of mutual fear.

18. Anthony Quinton, *Francis Bacon,* p. 9.

19. *Leviathan,* xlvi.

20. See his *Elements of Philosophy,* I.i.6. This theme is developed at length by John Dewey in "The Motivation of Hobbes' Political Philosophy," in *Thomas Hobbes in His Time,* ed. Ralph Ross, H. W. Schneider, and T. Waldman (Univ. of Minnesota Press, 1974). See also H. W. Schneider on "The Piety of Hobbes" in the same volume.

21. *De Cive,* Dedicatory Letter, pp. 10-11. Cp. Jean Hampton, *Hobbes and the Social Contract Tradition* (Cambridge Univ. Press, 1986), ch. 1.

I set down for a principle by experience known to all men, and denied by none, to wit, that the dispositions of men are naturally such, that except they be restrained through fear of some coercive power, every man will distrust and dread each other, and as by natural right he may, so by necessity he will be forced to make use of the strength he hath toward the preservation of himself.[22]

And again:

the state of men without civil society (which state we may properly call the state of nature) is nothing else but a mere war of all against all; and in that war all men have equal right to all things.[23]

He does not go so far as to claim that every person in every action is motivated entirely by self-interest, as if no shred of altruism exists, but lists among the human passions not only benevolence, goodwill, kindness, and charity but also indignation at hurt done to others.[24]

both sayings are very true: that man to man is a kind of God; and that man to man is an arrant wolf. The first is true if we compare citizens amongst themselves; and the second, if we compare cities. In the one, there is some analogy of similitude with the Deity, to wit justice and charity, the twin sisters of peace. But in the other, good men must defeat themselves by taking to them for a sanctuary the two daughters of war, deceit and violence: that is, in plain terms, a mere brutal rapacity.[25]

The cause of both religious and political conflicts, then, is found in the nature of individuals, but what then causes individuals to be the way they are? In the *Leviathan,* this is the prior question before Hobbes looks at individual behaviors and then recomposes them into a civil society; for the human being is, in his analysis, both the matter and maker of the state. It soon becomes evident that his scientific method of seeking constituent causes for human behavior commits him both to determinism and to a methodological materialism. The initial cause of all knowledge is sensations, produced by external physical causes of

22. *De Cive,* p. 11.
23. *De Cive,* p. 13.
24. *Leviathan,* vii.
25. *De Cive,* pp. 1f.

our brain processes. As those processes subside, after-images occur in both memory and dreams; subsequent brain processes cause ideas to combine in what we call "reasoning." All mental processes are physically caused; so too are our passions and actions. The appearance of freedom of the will arises because, in considering the consequences of a choice, we are conscious of alternating between two ideas until one weighs more heavily and the die is cast.

Science is knowledge of causes and consequences, logically demonstrated from empirical premises. Hobbes's list of the sciences ranges from mathematics to ethics and logic and, finally, the "science of just and unjust" that he is attempting to establish.[26] Theology is not included in this list, for in theology we have no "scientific" knowledge. It seems natural to believe in the existence of God as first cause, however, for the fear of things unknown causes us to imagine there are invisible powers. This is the "seed of religion" (a phrase used earlier by Calvin), and it is unique to human beings because we alone reason about causes. But any knowledge of God beyond this imaginative idea of a first cause depends on revelation. This separation of theology from philosophy and science will be crucial to Hobbes's recomposition of the church/state relationship.

Underlying his conception of science is Hobbes's explicit adoption of nominalism and its conception of "right reason." Both Scholastic appeals to abstract ideas and the private judgments of sectarians lack right reason, in that they use words lacking empirical definition. Words do not themselves signify anything but ideas, and language is merely a connection of words constituted by the will of their users to stand for certain ideas. Since we have no abstract universal ideas, universal terms are simply general names used indiscriminately in referring to similar images. By connecting words we form propositions. Every proposition that is universally true is either itself a definition, or else the evidence for it depends on a definition. Science, which is right reasoning, concerns itself with the truth of these general propositions or their logical consequences.[27] Wrong

---

26. *Leviathan,* ix.

27. *Leviathan,* iv; *Elements of Philosophy,* I.ii and iii. Michael Oakeshott maintains that this idea about the nature of right reasoning, inherited from Scotus and Ockham, is the driving force behind Hobbes's work. See his introduction to Hobbes's *Leviathan* (Blackwell, 1957). Hobbes claims to derive civil authority "from the nature of men, known to us by experience, and from the definition of such words as are essential to all political meaning" (*Leviathan,* xxxii).

reasoning misuses words, whether by arbitrary or false definition or by failing to see the consequences of the definitions we assert. It is wrong, then, to think of natural laws as commanding something, when they can only define or describe, or at most tell us what is prudent in the light of consequences. Laws have no authority in themselves. They can tell us it does not pay to cheat or steal because of the natural outcomes of such actions, but not because of divine punishment (for which no rational proof is possible), nor because they hurt the conscience (which has no coercive force in Hobbes's moral psychology).[28] Laws are nothing but the spoken definitions of those who command, be they human or divine.

We may distinguish three kinds of law: laws of nature, civil laws, and the law of God.

> A law of nature, *lex naturalis,* is a precept or general rule, found out by reason, by which a man is forbidden to do that which is destructive of his life, or taketh away means of preserving the same; and to omit that by which he thinketh it may be best preserved.[29]

Hobbes's definition is based on the fact that in the state of nature people are governed by their own reason, and are free to do whatever they think best for survival. This prudential thinking lies behind the general rule Hobbes calls the first law of nature:

> that each man ought to endeavor peace as far as he has hope of obtaining it; and when he cannot obtain it, that he may seek and use all helps and advantages of war.

A second law of nature follows from the first, that we should be willing for the sake of peace to covenant with others of like mind to limit our mutual liberties and transfer their rights to another. This is the basis for civil authority, and it implies a third law: that we keep the covenants we make. Keeping covenants is the meaning and source of justice, which is therefore only possible when there are authorities to enforce them. These and other virtues like gratitude and modesty all contribute to peace, and are thus desirable. Together they constitute a moral philosophy Hobbes sums up in the rule "do to others as we would be done

---

28. See G. S. Kavka, "Right Reason and Natural Law in Hobbes' Ethics," *Monist* 56 (1983): 120.

29. *Leviathan,* xiv.

to."[30] They are not absolute values, but simply prudential ones for the sake of peace and security. Justice, benevolence, friendship, and love are valued simply for their consequences.[31] This is a far remove from either Thomistic or Stoic natural law.

Civil laws are binding because we renounce our individual rights to do what we think necessary for our own protection, transferring them to a sovereign authority who will exercise power for the common good. We are therefore bound by this covenant to observe civil laws under penalty of punishment. Civil law consists of

> those rules, which the commonwealth hath commanded . . . to make use of, for the distinction of right and wrong; that is to say, of what is contrary, and what is not contrary to the rule.[32]

They are rules of what is just and unjust; nothing is unjust that is not contrary to civil law.

This equation of the just and right with civil law is crucial, for it rules out private judgment in moral matters and so precludes partisan disputes. Civil law and the laws of nature are coextensive, each containing the other, for performance of covenant is both a law of nature and a political obligation.

What civil law contributes is twofold. First, while natural law forbids theft and murder because of their social consequences, civil law defines what are to count as theft and murder under the terms of the covenant.[33] Second, civil law gives to natural law the force of law. Civil law does not derive its authority from natural law, as was the case in Aquinas's thinking, but natural law gains authority from civil law. Justice and moral obligation with respect to right and wrong begin when there is civil authority, not before. There is a prior distinction between the right and wrong things to do *prudentially*, in that peace is more useful than war. But this does not mean that some things are right or wrong in themselves, *unconditionally*, nor that the right is something I am *obligated* to do. The sovereign alone exercises such authority. This is a contractarian basis for ethics and a positivist theory of law; law is what the sovereign lays down and enforces.

30. *Leviathan,* xv and xvi.
31. *On Man,* ch. 11.
32. *Leviathan,* xxvi.
33. *De Cive,* vi.16.

What then about the law of God? For Aquinas, natural law promulgates the eternal law of God, and civil law applies natural law to a particular society. How then does Hobbes relate God to the law of nature, and the law of God to civil authority? Plainly these were the crucial questions in his historical situation. In *De Cive,* he observes that since the sovereign must be obeyed "in all things which repugn not the commandments of God," we need to know which are the laws and commandments of God. The laws of God are declared in three ways: by the tacit dictates of right reason, by immediate revelation, and by a prophet whom God recommends by means of miracles. The second way has occurred only occasionally and has not provided universal laws. The third is addressed to a chosen people in God's spiritual kingdom. But the first, right reason, is common to all and is therefore the way God rules his natural kingdom.[34] Hobbes shows Ockham's influence again by thus appealing to right reason and the Scriptures.

In the natural kingdom, right reason establishes laws regarding religion, and sectarian disputes are to be subdued by the right reason of the sovereign. Public worship of a uniform sort should be commanded throughout a commonwealth, and the sovereign must decide what the divine attributes are, how they should be honored, and by what actions. Likewise, disputes about why we believe Scripture to have divine authority must be settled by the sovereign. Insofar as the Scriptures coincide with the laws of nature, they are doubtless the unchanging law of God; but in other regards we accept their authority only on the authority of the sovereign.[35]

It follows that in the care of a Christian commonwealth, the authority of the church is in reality the authority of the state. God's natural kingdom and spiritual kingdom are one and the same. The words "temporal" and "spiritual," when used of government, "make men see double, and mistake their lawful sovereign." There can be only one sovereign ruler in this life, and there can be no lawful teaching of any doctrine that he does not allow as governor of both the state and religion. The alternative to this Erastian position is factionalism and civil war.[36] Hobbes is plainly addressing both the sectarians and the church authorities of his own troubled times. In fact, the concluding

34. *De Cive,* xv; *Leviathan,* xxxi.
35. *Leviathan,* xxxiii.
36. *Leviathan,* xxxix.

part IV of his *Leviathan* includes papal authority and various Roman Catholic beliefs and practices among errors stemming from the "kingdom of darkness." "Essences and substantial forms" receive the same treatment, as do the right to private judgment about laws, both natural and divine. Right reason prudently excludes them all.

The reception Hobbes's work received was understandably negative. Religious authorities objected, and "Hobbism" was also attacked for its materialism, its egoism, and its pessimistic view of human nature. We shall see something of this reaction in the next chapter. Some recent scholarship interprets Hobbes as combining the Christian natural law tradition with a divine command theory in a way that is incompatible with his mechanistic science.[37] Yet his nominalist rejection of Aristotelianism plainly supports an empirical approach to human nature and the science of his day. The result is a prudential, contractarian ethic and legal positivism that push the roles of right reason and divine law far beyond what Scotus and Ockham could have envisioned. God is no longer the good of contemplative devotion, but more the giver of laws mediated to us by right reason in the state. Theology is separated from science and philosophy, only to be governed by a political prudence informed by the causes and consequences known through modern science. As a result, science assumes the authority the church lost, and takes the place of metaphysics and theology in seeking grounds for ethics. No intrinsic connection between fact and value survives.

37. M. Cranston and R. S. Peters, *Hobbes and Rousseau: A Collection of Critical Essays* (Anchor Books, 1972). *Per contra* see Hampton, *Hobbes and the Social Contract Tradition;* Michael Oakeshott, *Hobbes on Civil Association* (Univ. of California Press, 1975).

CHAPTER NINE

Human Nature and Moral Teleology

THE *via moderna* of Ockham, we have seen, combined with mechanistic science to eliminate natural teleology. Being is not intrinsically good but is value-free; fact and value are separated. Immanuel Kant sums this up when, in objecting to the ontological argument, he declares that being is not a proper predicate. The rejection of Scholasticism had stripped being of its transcendental attributes, and left only bare facts, purposeless and dead. "Can I take a thing so dead?" asked Tennyson, "embrace it for my mortal good?"

In such a universe the aim of human reason is the attainment not of virtue but of power, power over nature's resources and power over ourselves. The motivation is not love of intrinsic good but desire for extrinsic goods — the pleasures of safety or satisfied wants. There are no intrinsic goods and no intrinsic rights. For Hobbes, the right is simply what the lawgiver says it is, an artificial and not a natural right at all.

This Hobbesian outcome evoked opposition from almost every quarter. Some seemingly agreed with his empirical approach and utilitarian direction, but objected to his pessimistic view of human nature. Others deplored the modern way as a whole — its epistemology, its artificial values, its extrinsic motivation, its lack of belief in an inner telos. Of the former sort are Locke and Hume. Of the latter sort are the Cambridge Platonists, the moral sense philosophers, and the Scottish realists. But all of them agreed on one thing: what we say about human nature is fundamental to any moral theory. In Pope's immortal words, "the proper study of mankind is man." The present chapter, then, is concerned with these reactions and the underlying moral psychologies.

The empiricist and determinist trend was wholly unacceptable to the Platonic thinkers centered at Cambridge.[1] Francis Bacon had deliberately separated philosophy from theology and relegated discussions of purpose to the theologians. Right reason in ethics would from then on look to empirical science. Thomas Hobbes took a natural next step. In a mechanistic world, human nature is like the rest of nature; our behavior is causally determined like everything else, and any social ethic or political order must depend on the edicts of rulers. John Smith and Benjamin Whichcote attacked this trend before Hobbes was recognized as a threat, while Ralph Cudworth and Henry More directed their attack at Hobbes himself. Nothing could be further from Plato, Plotinus, and Christian Neoplatonism than the view that humans do not naturally love the good; that they have no inner light that guides to truth, but rather depend for truth and goodness on sense experience.

The extreme Calvinism of some of the Puritans was equally objectionable. While Calvinist influence declined with the restoration of the Stuart monarchy in 1660, the antagonism of the Cambridge Platonists did not. They deplored sectarian disputes between Calvinists and Lutherans, which to the Platonist mind arose from ignoring the knowledge of God and the good vouchsafed by the light of reason. They rejected theologies that denied any inherent *eros* for truth and goodness, expected nothing from human reason, and derived morality solely from revealed laws of God imposed by sovereigns to enforce right conduct. Such a theology denigrated human nature and left no room for philosophy at all.

In contrast to Hobbes and the extreme Calvinists, Cudworth and More maintained that objective moral distinctions between right and wrong are rooted in the nature of things and can be discerned by the light of reason. God is the One, the Good, from whom flows the

---

1. On Cambridge Platonism, see Ernst Cassirer, *The Platonic Renaissance in England,* trans. J. P. Pettegrove (Univ. of Texas Press, 1953); Gerald R. Cragg, ed., *The Cambridge Platonists* (Oxford Univ. Press, 1968); J. H. Muirhead, *The Platonic Tradition in Anglo-Saxon Philosophy* (Macmillan, 1931); C. A. Patrides, ed., *The Cambridge Platonists* (Harvard Univ. Press, 1970).

ordered unity of the natural and spiritual worlds. The divine Logos, the orderer of creation, is the light of the world, God present in the human soul. The Platonic *eros,* the higher love within us, naturally seeks goodness and truth, and in doing so seeks God himself. Wrote Henry More of the human soul that sets it affections on things above:

> Not streaked with gaudy multiplicity,
> Pure light without discoloration,
> Stable without circumvolution,
> Eternal rest, joy without passing sound;
> What sound is made without collision?
> Smell, taste, and touch make God a gross compound,
> Yet truth of that that's good is perfectly here found.[2]

Moral distinctions, then, are rooted in a human nature constituted so as to distinguish higher from lower loves. Because the spirit of man is the candle of the Lord, moral knowledge comes ultimately from God, but to apprehend this knowledge we must love truth and goodness. For them Titus 2:11-12 summed up the essence of Christianity:

> For the grace of God that bringeth salvation hath appeared to all men, teaching us that, denying ungodliness and worldly lusts, we should live soberly, righteously, and godly in this present world.

Within this combination of Platonic philosophy and Christian theology, fact and value remain intrinsically united. Being is still good, whatever mechanistic science says about it and however the love for worldly things obscures its goodness. A pervasive teleology still gives to human nature its natural bent.

But in John Locke a very different story emerges. No inherent teleology draws us towards either truth or goodness.[3] The mind is declared to be a passive *tabula rasa.* Innate ideas are out of the question, and even the simple ideas that comprise our mental experience come as disconnected atoms of thought devoid of internal relations either to one another or to our past and future. Complex ideas are of our own making, and so are abstract ones. Similarly with goodness. Instead of

2. *Psychathanasia,* quoted by Cassirer, *Platonic Renaissance,* p. 65.
3. See Charles Taylor, *Sources of the Self* (Harvard Univ. Press, 1989), pp. 165-71.

innate ideas or an *eros* for God and the good, we are left with only the extrinsic motivation of pleasure and pain. Locke unwittingly prepares the way for hedonistic and utilitarian ethics.

This was not his intention, for he repeatedly talks about natural moral laws resting on the will of the Creator. While a "Hobbist" would say a man should keep his word "because the public requires it, and the Leviathan will punish you if you do not," a Christian should do so because "*God*, who has the power of eternal life and death, requires it of us."[4]

Locke had Calvinist roots; his father was one of the original signers of the Westminster Confession of Faith, and his *First Treatise on Civil Government* was directed against the paternalist theory of Robert Filmer — that a king's "divine right" to absolute authority is inherited from Adam, the father of our race. No such divine right exists, argues Locke. Rather, as the *Second Treatise* claims, power and civil authority rest on the equal rights of all rational beings to life, liberty, and property. God's will is evident in how he made us, so that natural law is simply a law promulgated by God in a natural way. His decree is discernible by the light of nature, which indicates what is and what is not in conformity with our rational powers.[5]

But there are no innate ideas of morality. Directing his famous rejection of this doctrine against the Cambridge Platonists, Locke says, rather, "nature has put into man a desire of happiness and an aversion to misery." This desire inclines us to the good, providing pleasure and pain as divine sanctions to motivate us and drive us into society.[6] Virtue is conjoined to public happiness.

Locke's empiricism is evident in his account of our moral knowledge. He distinguishes three degrees of knowledge: the intuitive, demonstrative, and sensory. All three kinds involve perception of the agreement or disagreement of ideas. Moral knowledge perceives agreement or disagreement between the idea of some voluntary action and the idea of

4. *Essay Concerning Human Understanding*, I.ii.5. See W. M. Spellman, *John Locke and the Problem of Depravity* (Clarendon, 1988), for a rigorous defense of Locke as a Broad Churchman, dissatisfied with both Pelagian and Puritan views of human nature.

5. *Essays on the Law of Nature*, ed. W. von Leyden (Clarendon, 1954), p. 111.

6. *Human Understanding*, I.ii.2, 6; *Second Treatise of Civil Government*, 77. This appeal to the extrinsic constraint of pleasure and pain is absent in Locke's earlier *Essays on the Law of Nature*.

moral law. Moral knowledge, like mathematics, depends on demonstration and therefore on intervening concepts in the argument.[7] To say, for example, that I violate the moral law by stealing someone's property, is to say that the idea of stealing conflicts with a moral rule concerning property. But this involves an abstract moral idea of right, or justice. Such an idea is an "archetype," the norm by which we make moral judgments like "stealing is wrong" and "a thief ought to be punished." Justice is an abstract idea, not one we can derive from empirical observations, so the essence of justice has to be established by definition. Yet if we all made up our own definitions, social chaos would result: think of the mathematical chaos if we all defined a triangle any way we wished. Moral ideas must therefore be unequivocally defined.

> Where God or any other lawmaker hath defined any moral name, there they have made the essence of that species to which that name belongs.[8]

Locke happens to be convinced, of course, that God has defined justice and promulgated the idea in the way he made us, that is to say, in human nature.

We thus need a further intermediate idea to make moral demonstration possible, an idea of human nature in general. Locke gets at this in both his *Essay Concerning Human Understanding* and his *Treatises of Civil Government*. In the former he abstracts the idea of a person from human experience. There is no real essence of persons or any other class of things, for Locke is a conceptualist, not a realist about universals. Abstraction from experience only yields a nominal essence that defines the idea sufficiently for the purposes of moral knowledge. Wherein does the identity of a person, the moral agent, consist? A person is a conscious, thinking, intelligent being, the same in different times and places. Continuity of consciousness is thus the key to moral reasoning; it is not necessary to assert the existence of some unchanging soul-substance, for continued identity of the one consciousness makes it just to punish or reward a person for past deeds.

> All the great ends of morality and religion are well enough secured, without philosophical proofs of the soul's immateriality; since it is

7. *Human Understanding*, III.xi.16-18; IV.xii.8; *Law of Nature*, Essay 2.
8. *Human Understanding*, IV.iv.10.

evident that, he who made us at the beginning to subsist here, sensible, intelligent beings, and for several years continued us in such a state, can and will restore us to the state of sensibility in another world, and makes us capable there to receive the retribution he has designed to men, according to their doings in this life.[9]

This idea of personal identity is all that demonstrative moral knowledge requires: no metaphysical account is needed.

The *Second Treatise* defines the morally significant idea of human nature by hypothesizing an original state in which all persons are equally free, ruled only by their reason. They are all equally God's property, creatures, and servants; none is superior to any other, and accordingly it is against the law of nature to invade others' rights.[10] The two accounts complement each other; the *Essay* says how I can be responsible for my past actions, while the *Treatise* says why I should not mistreat other people. Both accounts are needed for a complete ethic, but the *Treatise* opens the way to defining justice.

Hobbes made the idea of justice the result of a social covenant, an artificial rather than a natural thing. Locke, however, finds a moral right to property inherent in the state of nature. Natural law is the law of justice. John Dunn suggests that the key to this moral vision is the Calvinist concept of God's calling, which gives each person a work and a place in society. The value of work and of the property it provides stems from this vocation.[11] The *Second Treatise* accordingly begins by affirming that originally all people were equal and had "perfect freedom to order their actions and dispose of their possessions as they think fit within the bounds of the law of nature." It follows logically that no one ought to harm another's "life, health, liberty, or possessions." The basis is clear: we are God's workmanship, not our own, and our lives and work are a God-given vocation.

Locke appeals both to reason and to Scripture. The idea of property is of a right to have something, and injustice is by definition the invasion of a right.[12] God has entrusted the world to us in common, to use by industry and reason for our support and comfort; so it is

9. *Human Understanding*, IV.iii.6; cp. II.xxvii.7-11; xxviii.
10. *Second Treatise*, 4.
11. John Dunn, *The Political Thought of John Locke* (Cambridge Univ. Press, 1969), p. 245.
12. *Human Understanding*, IV.iii.18.

labor that lays claim to property. Moreover, since life and labor are to fulfill God's calling, property is "not for the fancy or covetousness of the quarrelsome and contentious."[13] It is given to all, not just a few, and it is an offense against natural law to take more than one can rightly use, or to harvest the fruit of one's labor and then let it rot. Labor can only claim a right to property that will be used for the human good. Justice is then the preservation of God-given natural rights to life, liberty, and property, and the function of civil government is to uphold justice by the rule of laws applied equally to rich and poor, powerful and powerless alike. Not only the authority and functions of government but the limitations of political authority are therefore ultimately derived from natural law evident in us as rational beings, equally free to live our own lives and dispose of our possessions. Government, in this sense — not in Filmer's paternalist sense or Hobbes's more artificial sense — is ordained by God.

Locke's definition of justice in terms of the natural rights of rational human beings did not satisfy David Hume, who fifty years later wrote his *A Treatise of Human Nature.* Rejecting abstract ideas like that of justice, he took a more thoroughly empirical, psychological approach to human nature. He was not convinced that objective values are independent of human nature, nor that reason can either make demonstrative moral judgments or motivate the moral life, nor that the civil society arises from a hypothetical contract among rational individuals. These issues were also being debated by the moral sense philosophers, who were not ready to accept the mechanistic philosophy and the *via moderna* underlying Hobbes's work, and especially not the view that nature is itself value-free, devoid of inner teleology or natural good. Scottish thought, still influenced by Aristotelianism, resisted this conclusion and sought ways to affirm a natural moral *telos* and objective values. Others were content to argue for a natural benevolence in human beings, in contrast to Hobbes's egoistic tendencies.

One of these moral sense philosophers was the Earl of Shaftesbury, a former student of Locke's, who thought his mentor's insistence on demonstrative moral knowledge undercut commonsense morality. Rather, introspection reveals a natural benevolent sentiment that distinguishes right from wrong. Frances Hutcheson found evidence of a natural desire for other people's happiness in the fact that we spon-

13. *Second Treatise*, 34.

taneously approve actions with benevolent motives and disapprove others. This is an involuntary response to our moral perceptions. Hume met Hutcheson after completing his *Treatise* and gave more attention to benevolence in his later *Enquiry Concerning the Principles of Morals.* But both of these works share the general approach of moral sense philosophy.[14]

Hume, however, had read Locke but moved closer to Ockham than to Aristotle. He was deeply impressed by Newton's scientific method of analysis and reconstruction. Recognizing that a moral sense theory must be grounded in psychology, he decided to investigate human nature using Newton's method. The original title page of his *A Treatise of Human Nature* bore the subtitle "being an attempt to introduce the experimental method of reasoning into moral subjects." The outcome, he wrote, is

> a compleat system of the sciences, built on a foundation almost entirely new, and the only one upon which they can stand with any security.[15]

It is not a metaphysic but an empirical science of human nature that is to provide the foundation for ethics. How objective the method is and how adequate an account it yields may well be debated. Because of his aversion to Aristotelianism as well as his empirical method, human nature has no fixed essence; while we are only what nature has made us, culture is also an influence to be reckoned with in any empirical account. Alasdair MacIntyre declares the resultant view of human nature to be one variant of the eighteenth-century English country gentlemen Hume was doubtless acquainted with.[16]

But what does the empirical science of human nature show? First, human nature has certain universal proclivities by virtue of which

---

14. For discussion of Hume's relation to these moral sense philosophers, see David F. Norton, *David Hume: Common Sense Moralist, Skeptical Metaphysician* (Princeton Univ. Press, 1982), ch. 1; J. L. Mackie, *Hume's Moral Theory* (Routledge & Kegan Paul, 1980), ch. 2; Stanley Tweyman, *Reason and Conduct in Hume and His Predecessors* (Nijhoff, 1974).

15. *A Treatise of Human Nature,* ed. L. A. Selby-Bigge (Clarendon, 1888), p. xx.

16. Alasdair MacIntyre, *Whose Justice? Which Rationality?* (Univ. of Notre Dame Press, 1988), p. 295.

there are things we naturally believe, and moral feelings we naturally experience. Hume is a critic of Enlightenment epistemology, its quest for certainty, and its claim that humans are primarily rational beings ruled by reason in what they believe and do. His skepticism about knowledge of matters of fact opens the way to a psychology of belief and a moral psychology based on empirically observable proclivities of human nature.[17]

Second, as this implies, it is not reason but the passions that are the source of both belief and morality. An inferred belief is a response to external causes that repeatedly conjoin similar ideas. It is a mental habit, distinguished from mere imagination by a sentiment we feel — a vivid, forcible, and steady impression that something is the case. It is as unavoidable as the passion of love or hatred, a kind of natural instinct that no reasoning process can either produce or prevent.[18] Such passions are determined by the constitution of the mind, for "nature has bestowed a kind of attraction on certain impressions and ideas" and "has given to the organs of the human mind a certain disposition fitted to produce" particular emotions in response to perceptions.[19] Moral approval and disapproval are just such inner impressions, and moral distinctions are derived from these feelings rather than by any rational process. Not only moral judgments but moral conduct also is similarly caused, for reason alone cannot affect behavior.

Locke had recognized the need for pleasure and pain as external sanctions to motivate some people to moral behavior, but his insistence on demonstrative moral knowledge is altogether unacceptable to Hume. At the root of this is their disagreement about the basic constituents of perception. Locke analyzes experience into clear and distinct ideas of sensation and reflection, as if it were an objective and entirely unfeeling thing, while Hume traces ideas to forceful and vivacious impressions of an affective sort. External impressions give rise to ideas that in turn can give rise to other internal impressions. Experience is basically

17. See N. K. Smith, *The Philosophy of David Hume* (Macmillan, 1941), and more recently James Noxon, *Hume's Philosophical Development* (Clarendon, 1973); Annette C. Baier, *A Progress of Sentiments* (Harvard Univ. Press, 1991); and N. Capaldi, J. King, and D. Livingston, "The Hume Literature of the 1980's," *American Philosophical Quarterly* 28 (1991): 225.

18. *An Inquiry Concerning Human Understanding,* V.

19. *Treatise,* II.i.5.

Hume

passional, and only secondarily cognitive. Moral passions are secondary, internal impressions of reflection. Reason only influences conduct when it provides the idea of a particular object that excites passion, or when it shows a causal connection by which a passion is aroused.[20]

But demonstrative moral knowledge is impossible also because it depends on abstract ideas and Hume is a nominalist, rejecting abstract ideas. Our knowledge is limited to relations of ideas (analytic judgments) and to matters of fact that are empirically accessible. Normative moral judgments that employ abstract ideas like justice can be of neither sort; they are not judgments at all.

Of particular interest here is Hume's insistence that moral qualities are not matters of objective fact independent of human experience, but pertain rather to the relation between external objects and internal states of mind. They are not, like Locke's primary qualities, properties of the objects themselves. Hume likens them instead to secondary qualities that arise in the mind from the interaction between external objects and the self. Morality is indeed grounded in nature, and so Hume is an ethical naturalist; but it is on natural passional experience, not on some other independent or cosmic reality, that it depends.

Moral distinctions arise from impressions and involve pleasure or pain. Desire and aversion are directly caused by pleasure or pain. Pride and humility are caused indirectly by way of pleasing or distasteful ideas about oneself. Similarly, love and hatred are related to ideas we have of others. All of these feelings — desire and aversion, pride and humility, love and hate — are passions; and it is here that moral distinctions must arise if there are to be compelling moral feelings.[21]

pain pleasure drives

Hume accordingly treats justice as self-regarding rather than entirely altruistic.[22] When I observe the sufferings of others and infer their cause, I connect their experience to myself because of our relationship to each other or our similarities. This association of ideas produces painful impressions, and the sympathy I feel causes me to disapprove whatever causes the pain and approve what alleviates it. This is a matter

---

20. *Treatise,* III.i.1-2.

21. *Treatise,* II.i.7; iii.9; III.iii.1.

22. For Hume's theory of justice, see *Treatise,* III.ii; *Enquiry Concerning the Principles of Morals,* iii-iv and Appendix iii; *Essays, Moral, Political and Literary* in vol. 2 of *The Philosophical Works of David Hume,* ed. T. H. Green and T. H. Grose (Longman, Green, 1898)

of common interest, the public good. We name "just" what has desirable utility in this way, and call "unjust" what is undesirable.

Whereas in the *Treatise* Hume denies there is any such natural passion as love of mankind or disinterested benevolence, his *Enquiry Concerning the Principles of Morals* asserts that there is, and he bases moral distinctions on it.[23] Self-love cannot make moral distinctions because it produces different sentiments in different people, but benevolence produces the same sentiments in everyone. Benevolence is a natural passion, universally approving or disapproving some things. There is no longer need for the association of ideas to intervene. Rather, we observe the suffering of other people, and benevolence approves whatever has utility in alleviating their distress.

Justice and injustice are simply terms we have invented to express this moral distinction. Since justice is not a natural idea arising directly from our sense impressions, but an artificial one, we can define how the term is to be used and derive particular moral precepts from its meaning.[24] Yet although justice is an artificial idea, its precepts are not arbitrary but may in fact be regarded as "laws of nature," rooted as they are in human nature.

As human beings we have numberless wants and necessities and few means of supplying them alone. We remedy this natural condition by combining our resources and abilities. We see this in the family with its endearing ties, but since these ties are lacking in society at large we have to devise ways of ensuring that resources will be available to meet our needs. We adopt rules about property for stability of possession; ownership should be transferable only by consent, and we must do what we promise. Thus arise moral rules, precepts of justice, as conventions about property. The laws of nations are but an extension of these conventions to relationships between governments, and arise because, where possession has no stability, perpetual war results. Where property is not transferred by consent, commerce is impossible; where promises are not kept, no alliances are made.[25] Laws of nations are not like contracts we promise to keep, despite what Hobbes claims, for promising is not prior to them but arises from them. They are natural laws because of their utility; human nature being as it is, they

23. Cp. *Treatise*, III.ii.1 and *Enquiry*, ii.
24. *Essays*, XXIII.
25. Cp. *Enquiry*, Appendix III; *Essays*, IV and V.

arise naturally. It is enlightened self-interest that constructs such a system.]

At first glance, Hume has moved little beyond Hobbes. Even though his emphasis on natural benevolence in the *Enquiry* suggests a more optimistic view of human nature, and he says a "war of all against all" is not our original state since we are born and reared in families, yet justice is still necessary "for peace, safety and mutual intercourse."[26] Hobbes and Hume differ over whether justice originates from a covenant, and over the roles of reason and passion, but their main difference is over property. Hobbes assumes it already existed in the state of nature; for Hume, property is something we invent as a matter of utility. This is true also of marriage:

> The long and helpless infancy of man requires the combination of parents for the subsistence of their young, and that combination requires the virtue of chastity or fidelity to the marriage bed. Without such a *utility*, it will readily be owned that such a virtue would never have been thought of. . . . Common interest and utility beget infallibly a standard of right and wrong among the parties concerned.[27]

This was hardly enough to satisfy the more traditional advocates of natural law, in particular Hume's fellow Scots. With their Calvinist theology, they regarded the existing property rules as unjust, because justice is both antecedent to property and a natural rather than artificial idea. Hume had been taught all this as a law student, and had read natural law advocates like Hugo Grotius and Samuel Pufendorf. But he compromised both his religious roots and his Scottish heritage in aligning himself with the landed English gentry, with the result that when he applied for a professorship at the University of Edinburgh, he was rejected. Subsequently, he justified the revolution of 1688 that overthrew the Stuart James II by pointing out the obvious — that the Stuarts no longer held power — and by denying that the Scottish Jacobite dynasty could possess a right independently of its possession of power.[28]

26. *Enquiry*, iii.
27. *Enquiry*, iv.
28. See Baier, *Progress of Sentiments*, pp. 225-27; J. B. Stewart, *The Moral and Political Philosophy of David Hume* (Columbia Univ. Press, 1963); MacIntyre, *Whose Justice?* chs. 12-16.

Hume's Scottish Presbyterian background echoes when he writes that the "constant conjunctions" between motive and action are in practice acknowledged both in the schools and in the pulpit.[29] Laws, whether human or divine, are enforced by rewards and punishments that produce good actions and prevent evil ones. He himself preferred a more gentle and liberal religion, something more akin to that of the English gentry, more deistic than Christian. He repeatedly refers to a divine Maker, speaking of reason as founded on the nature of things "by the will of the Supreme Being" and of moral sentiment likewise as "ultimately derived from that Supreme Will which bestowed on each being its peculiar nature, and arranged the several classes and orders of existence."[30]

> The universal propensity to believe in invisible, intelligent power . . . may be considered as a kind of mark or stamp, which the divine workman has set upon his work; and nothing surely can more dignify mankind, than to be thus selected from all other parts of creation and to bear the image or impression of the universal Creator.[31]

Our ideas about God, however, may be badly disfigured and entirely uncertain. "Speculative dogmas of religion" are suspect; a causal argument for God's existence can only point to a cause proportionate to its effect, and therefore can prove neither a perfect intelligence with perfect goodness, nor a future judge. Our ideas about God are not established by reason; they are more like an explanatory hypothesis than the logical conclusion of a proof.

How does this affect his ethic? In the *Dialogues Concerning Natural Religion,* Cleanthes claims that the doctrine of a future state with its rewards and punishments is a strong and necessary "security to morals."[32] Philo asks how, if that is so, all history abounds so much with civil wars, persecutions, oppression, and slavery — all of them often justified in the name of religion. True religion may be different, but reason cannot determine which is true. Hume questions any

---

29. *Treatise,* II.iii.2.

30. *Enquiry,* Appendix I. On this aspect of his thought, see Keith Yandell, *Hume's Inexplicable Mystery* (Temple Univ. Press, 1990).

31. *The Natural History of Religion,* xv.

32. *Dialogues,* xii.

morally effective connection between religion and morality, despite traditional preaching about heaven and hell.

But is there some other connection? After all, Hume refers to God as the source of both reason and moral sentiment. After denying that moral distinctions can be derived from reason, he adds that moralists seem to jump from "is" to "ought," and "is not" to "ought not," without giving a reason.[33] His point seems to be that the sense of moral compulsion, like our moral distinctions, is based in the passions, not in reason. But if the passions and their moral feelings come ultimately "from the Supreme Will," then our sense of moral compulsion is also willed by God. The move from "is" to "ought" may not be a direct inference, but granted this further premise about the divine source of moral feeling, and granted the constant conjunction between motive and action, then it appears to follow that God wills that our actions accord with moral feeling. The "is" comes already loaded with a sense of "ought." The term may be inappropriate for Hume because of his determinism, but the feeling of "ought" as explained within his account is, if we take his references to God at face value, God-given.

But for Hume the experimental method carries the day alone, and he assumes what later becomes the unity-of-science thesis. Understandably, then, observable regularities give rise to general laws about moral psychology, and explanatory hypotheses of a theological sort can hardly be included. Nor could he accept an active teleology inherent in human nature, such as the Medievals claimed. His is a more mechanistic picture of moral behavior caused by moral sentiments that are in turn caused by the passions. Hume plainly intends his ethic to be universally valid, since it is based on the general causal laws of human moral psychology. Subjectivist grounds can only imply a relativist ethic if the grounds are historically or individually relative. Yet Scottish philosophers retaining more of the Aristotelian emphasis on teleology, more of natural-law jurisprudence and a more traditional theism, took a different direction. Thomas Reid, the Scottish realist, is an outstanding example. He agrees with Hume in rejecting Locke's demonstrative moral knowledge along with the underlying theory of representational ideas. Such principles, he wrote to Hume,

33. *Treatise,* III.i.1.

I never thought of calling into question, until the conclusions you draw from them in *The Treatise of Human Nature* made me suspect them.[34]

Like Hume, he adopts Newton's method of observation and experiment for the study of human nature.

Conjectures and theories are the creatures of men, and will always be found very unlike the creatures of God. If we would know the works of God, we must consult them with attention and humility, without daring to add anything of ours to what they declare . . . whatever we add of our own is apocryphal, and of no authority.[35]

But beyond this beginning, disagreement with Hume becomes more and more frequent.

COUNTER — →Knowledge and belief do not always originate with simple im-
HUME pressions and ideas, and so Hume is wrong about the association of ideas. Factual knowledge does not always depend on causal inferences, nor does belief have to arise from constant conjunctions. Some judgments and beliefs precede or accompany perception; for instance, commonsense beliefs in the independent reality of material objects. A sensation we experience is not just a subjective mental state but is also a natural sign pointing to the external object. It has an external reference, a telos, an intentionality. Belief in material objects is then a spontaneous, natural belief, a first principle from which reasoning naturally and rightly proceeds. Moreover, we naturally abstract ideas from what we experience; it is not a matter of *imagining* the nature of something in abstraction from particulars, but of learning to speak and use language. Human nature is not something we imagine as stripped of all particular qualities, but something we talk about in general terms. Virtues and vices also can be precisely defined.

But this does not mean that, like Locke, we can logically deduce moral obligations from what we know of human nature.[36] They do indeed result from the constitution God has given us and the circumstances in which he places us, but both our nature and our circum-

34. Letter to David Hume, March 18, 1763, *The Works of Thomas Reid*, ed. Sir William Hamilton (Edinburgh, 1895), vol. 1, p. 91.
35. *An Inquiry into the Human Mind*, ch. 1, and p. 97.
36. *Essays on the Intellectual Powers of Man*, vii.2, and p. 478.

stances are contingent matters, not amenable to demonstrative knowledge. Neither they nor the obligations they bring are logically necessary. Moral knowledge is of two sorts: it is self-evident to everyone with a mature understanding and moral faculty, or else it is deduced from moral knowledge that is self-evident. A person without such a conscience is like someone color-blind, functionally impaired.

Moral belief, then, is not dependent on the passions alone, but far more on reason. Dugald Stewart would later add that differing moral opinions are just different applications of the same moral principles, applications due to different physical or social circumstances. Moral principles are universally self-evident to the mature and properly functioning mind.

Further, moral beliefs are not just ideas accompanied by forceful passions; they are judgments about what is objectively true. Hume does not talk in terms of moral truth or an objective moral order, but only of moral sentiments caused by subjective and self-referential passions. He treats love of truth as just another passion, one elicited by the pleasure of satisfied curiosity.[37] And he avoids talking of objective moral duty, offering a descriptive moral psychology rather than a basis for moral obligation. Reid remedies all of this with his more active teleology and theism. Morality, like all science, has first principles self-evident to everyone who has a conscience and has taken the pains to exercise it. Conscience is the law of God written in the heart; we cannot disobey it without acting unnaturally. It grows to maturity from an imperceptible seed planted by our Creator, and nature intends that it regulate our active desires.[38]

The self-evident principles are quite general. Some things merit approval, others blame, so we ought to use the best means we can to be well informed of our duty. We should prefer a greater good to a lesser; we should not do to others what we would think wrong if it were done to us. We ought to apply such principles in approving what someone does; what the person does may also give me a pleasant feeling, but the moral judgment is not reducible, semantically or grammatically, to a description of those feelings.[39]

Reid reintroduces moral duty by taking conscience to be the law

---

37. *Treatise,* II.iii.10.
38. *Essays on the Active Powers of the Human Mind,* vol. 2, p. 637.
39. *Essays on the Active Powers of the Human Mind,* I.5, III.iii.6.

of God written in the human heart. But duty, as Kant quickly saw, assumes freedom of the will. Here too Reid differs from Hume.[40] Moral judgments are rational acts not caused by our passions, for the will is active in every operation of the mind. There are things I can do if I will: I can pay attention, I can deliberate, I can resolve what I shall do, I can maintain a fixed purpose. Without such acts of will, nothing can be either virtuous or immoral, for a virtue is a habit, a fixed purpose of acting rightly. To exercise one's will in these ways is to be a moral agent.

Will is not passion

Hume's basic problem here is not only his determinism; it is his view of personal identity. While Locke claimed that the continuity of consciousness gives rise to the idea of one continuing self, Hume denies any such self-concept. We have no underlying impressions to give rise to such an idea, nor do we have any idea of a soul or whatever entity it is that continues to exist; all we know is a succession of impressions and ideas that appear and disappear like ghostly specters. With no idea of a self, there can be no idea of a moral agent who wills and acts and fulfills obligations. All we can know is our passions, impressions, and ideas. Reid's analysis of human nature includes *active* powers of the mind, its causal power to initiate what otherwise would not occur. This abstract idea, he claims, is held even by children, despite Hume's denial that we can have any idea of power at all. We are causal agents; our actions are not just passive effects of psychological causes that deny us all initiative.

Hume

What then happens to the concept of justice? Reid rejects the notion that it is an artificial virtue valued solely for its utility. It is a matter of conscience, rooted in the human constitution; it is a matter of duty, not just utility.

> What I maintain, is first, that when men come to the exercise of their moral faculty, they perceive a turpitude in injustice, as they do in other crimes, and consequently an obligation to justice, abstracting from the consideration of its utility. And secondly, that as soon as men have any rational conception of a favor, and of an injury, they must have the conception of justice, and perceive its obligation distinct from its utility.[41]

40. Cp. Hume's *Treatise*, I.iv.6, and Reid's *Active Powers*, Essay 1.
41. *Active Powers*, V.5, p. 653.

This is surely the kernel of Reid's argument against Hume. Moral indignation is evident even among those who, like robbers, have little active regard for the common good. Gratitude for favors only makes sense because a favor goes beyond what is just, and resentment for injury only because it falls short of justice. All these natural sentiments presuppose the idea of justice. Property rights likewise depend on it. A state of nature with property but no idea of justice would be impossible; Hume's state of nature would be the same as Hobbes's. But justice is a duty of conscience, a law of nature, the fixed purpose of giving to all their due and injuring no one. On this principle property rights and every other human right depend. Possession is not nine tenths of the law — not, at least, of the natural moral law of justice.

CHAPTER TEN

Kant's Moral Worldview

Like his predecessors, Immanuel Kant was compelled to relate his ethic to the world of mechanistic science. But rather than extending the methods of science to ethics, as they had done, he sought instead to limit the domain of science and present the natural order as part of a larger moral teleology. When he spoke of "doing away with knowledge to make room for faith," he meant by "faith" a moral worldview. The *Critique of Pure Reason* concludes with a preview of this moral faith. The *Critique of Practical Reason* postulates the existence of a moral deity and a personal immortality characterized above all by moral growth. The *Critique of Judgment* uncovers the moral teleology within both aesthetic experience and the natural order. Later writings develop the outlines of a teleological philosophy of history. Step by painstaking step, Kant unfolds his picture of a moral universe.[1]

Kant has been called the Protestant philosopher. If this label is warranted, it is because his theism is oriented not to contemplation but to moral duty. It does not begin with his moral argument for the existence of God, let alone depend on the questionable assumptions of more traditional proofs. Rather, it reflects Kant's basic conviction that a supersensible reality reveals itself in the moral consciousness. This is the overall context of Kant's thought, the context in which he grew up,

1. See Thomas Auxter, *Kant's Moral Teleology* (Mercer Univ. Press, 1982); R. Kroner, *Kant's Weltanschauung,* trans. John Smith (Univ. of Chicago Press, 1956); and Keith Ward, *The Development of Kant's View of Ethics* (Blackwell, 1972).

in which his philosophy took its earliest shape, and in which his ethical theory was forged. While it is a faith he acquired in a pietist upbringing, it is not itself a pietist faith; for the ongoing struggles of moral growth preclude a pious peace of mind and soul, and hope for continued growth in the hereafter prevents any pessimistic gloom over the irremediable condition of human nature. While nature dwarfs us, he suggests, the moral law gives a person dignity and value. Nature and moral law together define the human self.

> Two things fill the mind with ever new and increasing admiration and awe, the oftener and the more steadily we reflect on them: the starry heavens above me and the moral law within me. I do not merely conjecture them and seek them as though obscured in darkness or in the transcendent region beyond my horizon: I see them before me, and I associate them directly with the consciousness of my own existence.[2]

This view of the self reaches far beyond Descartes's dualism and Hume's denial of any enduring self in his "bundle of perceptions." Kant is aware that the natural order accounts for our desires and inclinations, but his focus is on the freedom to will what moral law requires. He drew on Rousseau's perception of the autonomous individual, free from domination by either natural circumstances or other people; for both Kant and Rousseau, the Enlightenment's freedom from authority meant individual autonomy.

> Enlightenment is man's release from his self-incurred tutelage. Tutelage is man's inability to make use of his understanding without direction from another. Self-incurred is this tutelage when its cause lies not in lack of reason but in lack of resolution and courage to use it without direction from another. *Supere aude!* Have courage to use your own reason! — that is the motto of Enlightenment.[3]

And again:

2. *Critique of Practical Reason,* trans. L. W. Beck (Bobbs-Merrill, 1956), p. 166.

3. *What Is Enlightenment?* p. 85 in the Bobbs-Merrill 1959 ed. of *Foundations of the Metaphysics of Morals,* trans. L. W. Beck. See J. Stout, *The Flight from Authority* (Univ. of Notre Dame Press, 1981).

The touchstone of everything that can be concluded as a law for a
people lies in the question whether the people could have imposed
such a law on itself.[4]

Freedom and the rule of reason, then, go hand in hand. Unless one
stands back, reflects, and acts deliberately, there really is no freedom
from authority and tradition. Nor is there freedom from the rush of
circumstances, the pressure of other people, or the demands of one's
own inner drives and desires.

Kant's method is to uncover the universal preconditions of morality.
This is the transcendental method he developed in the first *Critique*,
rather than any extension of scientific methods; his point is that freedom
is the precondition of morality. The moral consciousness tells us that the
only unqualified good is a good will, one that acts out of duty rather than
inclination.[5] By telling us this, it forces us to be aware of our own freedom
and responsibility in controlling our own actions. Autonomy of the will,
as distinct from heteronomy, is thus essential to Kant's ethic.

The will involves two elements: practical reason and the power
of choice. Reason's respect for moral law produces feelings of pain or
pleasure about the conformity or nonconformity of our actions to that
law, and these feelings are incentives to the power of choice. Yet the
choice is never wholly determined either by reason or by inclinations
and desires, for it always retains a spontaneity of its own.[6]

The will thus stands at the juncture of a formal principle, respect
for moral law, and a material principle, the incentive of moral feelings
produced by the moral law. In adopting as its maxim whatever respect
for duty requires, it reveals its love for the morally good rather than
for extraneous objects of desire. A good will that loves the good above
all else is the only thing unconditionally good. Loving the good does
not by itself make a particular action morally right; but it does provide
a material principle that helps reason define particular duties. Kant
bursts out with a hymn of praise!

Duty! Thou sublime and mighty name that dost embrace nothing
charming nor insinuating . . . a law before which all inclinations are

4. *What Is Enlightenment?* p. 89.
5. *Foundations*, sec. 1.
6. John Silber, Introduction to Kant's *Religion Within the Limits of Reason
Alone* (Harper Torchbooks, 1960), p. lxxxiii. Cp. *Practical Reason*, pp. 74-76.

dumb even though they secretly work against it: what origin is there worthy of thee, and where is to be found the root of thy noble descent . . . ?[7]

Thus, for right moral choice the object of desire is what duty requires. Virtue is its end, its telos. Cultivating mental and physical powers is but a means, not the end in itself. But cultivating moral virtue is an essential end,[8] because the person is an end of intrinsic worth and never just a means.[9] The ultimate ideal is a kingdom of ends — a systematic union of autonomous rational beings, each a sovereign willing universal laws to which everyone is subject out of respect for the dignity of everyone else, and not for personal advantage. A just society is one in which "the freedom of the will of each can coexist together with the freedom of everyone in accordance with a universal law."[10]

Kant distinguishes between a "supreme" and a "perfect" good.[11] A supreme good is both unconditionally good in itself and the necessary condition for any other good. Thus virtue is the supreme good; it is not only unconditionally good in itself, it is also the necessary condition for developing our own abilities or achieving a just society. On the other hand, a perfect good is the entire and complete good of rational beings; it includes not only virtue but happiness as well, the contentment of cultivating virtue and living in a just society, and a happiness proportionate to one's virtue. Virtue leads to happiness; but we gain happiness not by seeking to be happy but by seeking virtue. If virtue then is not rewarded with happiness in this life, it must be in the hereafter; and we must postulate a moral deity to guarantee this perfect good.

This is what Kant claims in his second *Critique*. But is this moral faith, this moral teleology, anything more than a mental construct? Does the will just seem to us to be free or is it really so? Will virtue really be rewarded with happiness? Does God really exist? In Kant's terminology, is it all merely phenomenal — mere appearance — or is it noumenal — independently real?

7. *Practical Reason*, p. 89.

8. *The Doctrine of Virtue*, pt. 2 of *The Metaphysics of Morals*, trans. Mary Gregor (Univ. of Pennsylvania Press, 1964), pt. 1, bk. 2.

9. *Foundations*, p. 47.

10. *The Metaphysical Elements of Justice*, pt. 1 of *The Metaphysics of Morals*, trans. John Ladd (Bobbs-Merrill, 1965), p. 35.

11. *The Metaphysical Elements*, pp. 114-17.

The idea of teleology, let alone a moral teleology in nature, was absent from mechanistic science. Bacon simply left questions of purpose to the theologians; Hobbes's methodology excluded them; Spinoza dismissed the very notion. In ethics, however, the moral sense philosophers and the Scottish realists asserted that our rational faculties and moral proclivities are designed by God to lead us to certain moral beliefs. Kant seems to agree. But does his epistemology allow it? Does he not do away with knowledge? Sense experience is made possible by the *a priori* form of space, and our inner awareness involves the *a priori* form of time. The way we understand experience is structured, in other words, by *a priori* categories; the entire unity of our conscious apprehension stems from the play of these subjective principles. As a result we only know things as they appear to us, phenomena, rather than things as they really are in themselves, noumena.

The outcome is that we run continually into logical problems. On the ethically crucial topic of human freedom, Kant finds himself faced with an antinomy: on the one hand, he finds proof for this freedom, but on the other hand he finds disproof. If everything in the world takes place according to the laws of nature, the notion of freedom is reduced to a transcendental idea. Logically, this transcendental idea cannot be made to fill the gaps in the causal description of human behavior. Yet the idea cannot be dispensed with.[12]

Kant does not let it rest there. In the *Foundations of the Metaphysics of Morals,* he contrasts two kinds of causality:

> As will is a kind of causality of living beings so far as they are rational, freedom would be that property of this causality by which it can be effective independently of foreign causes determining it, just as natural necessity is the property of causality of all irrational beings by which they are determined in their activity by the influence of foreign causes.[13]

12. This is the third conflict of ideas of the Transcendental Dialectic in his *Critique of Pure Reason.*

13. *Foundations,* p. 64. A similar line of thought appears in the *Practical Reason.* There Kant argues that natural phenomena are all temporal while noumena such as freedom of will are not. That is why a freely chosen action could have been left undone. Another kind of causation is at work, namely the free choice of the will that has no antecedent necessary cause but acts spontaneously.

Both kinds of causality operate under law: natural causality under the laws of nature, and freedom of will under the laws of morality. We must adopt different standpoints in thinking of them. The laws of morality are founded on reason independently of the phenomenal world of sense; they are freely self-imposed rather than subject to natural causes. Their ground, then, is the rational self that belongs to a real, supersensible world, rather than the world of sense and appearance. Freedom of will is thus supersensible, noumenal. On the other hand, we do not know the ground of natural causation; our knowledge of it is merely phenomenal. It is in moral choice and action that the reality of a supersensible world is revealed. For unless such a supersensible world exists, no moral incentive is conceivable; there would be no causal connection between virtue and happiness, and we could not explain pangs of conscience about past actions that could have been avoided.

From the purely theoretical standpoint of the first *Critique,* then, the idea of freedom had only regulative value as a possible way of accounting for the lack of known causes. From the standpoint of practical reason, however, the reality of a supersensible world is now definitely established as firmly known.[14] A world that is known independently of sense experience is known independently of the *a priori* forms and categories that limit us to the phenomenal. The self is truly free when it acts under the rule of reason alone.

It is in the supersensible world that both virtue and happiness are fully possible. In the world of sense, no rational being achieves mastery of all the inclinations and desires, as perfect virtue requires. Nor, in the world of sense, can there be complete contentment except through self-sufficiency in total independence of whatever it is we now desire. While only God is completely self-sufficient, progress for humans is possible — continually so if the rational self lives on after death. But we must postulate an immortality of the soul; and to explain how moral perfection is possible, we must postulate the existence of God. The practical necessity of a supersensible world extends to these two conclusions.

The connection is that God is the only being in whom holiness (*supreme* goodness) and self-sufficiency (*perfect* happiness) exist and are united. God is thus the moral ideal, his will is moral law, and he

14. *Practical Reason,* p. 109.

himself is the only adequate cause of our highest good — a happiness proportioned to virtue. It is morally necessary to assume the existence of God. "Love God above all and thy neighbor as thyself," Kant declared, agrees well with moral law. "To love God means to *like* to do his commandments, and to love one's neighbor means to *like* to practice all duties toward him."[15] And as he declared in his early *Lectures on Ethics,* what motivates the will to act morally is the belief that there is a judge of all things and an ultimate moral order in the universe.

This is the moral faith of which Kant spoke in his first *Critique.* It is not just the most reasonable opinion to hold: it is a moral duty to make the highest good the object of our will.

> Granted that the pure moral law inexorably binds every man as a command (not as a rule of prudence), the righteous man may say: I will that there be a God, that my existence in this world be also an existence in a pure world of the understanding outside the system of natural connections, and finally that my duration be endless. I stand by this and will not give up this belief. . . .[16]

This moral argument, it should be remembered, is not a deductive proof. It rather uncovers a presupposition already implicit in the obligation to act out of duty; implicit, that is, in ordinary moral consciousness. It appeals to rational coherence rather than to a chain of inference, but the connection is such that to deny God's existence is to undermine objective moral law.

It is a moral faith, Kant says. He regards both faith and knowledge as "valid for everyone," and there is "sufficient ground for holding them to be true"; the difference is that while knowledge is both objectively and subjectively sufficient, faith is only subjectively so.[17] It is necessary from a moral point of view, but not from a purely theoretical one. A moral faith is therefore not just assent to one or two propositions we could as readily deny, but a belief that in practice is necessary if we are to take the moral point of view seriously and consistently. It is an overall worldview in which God is the sole and self-sufficient ground of free-

15. *Practical Reason,* pp. 85-87.
16. *Practical Reason,* p. 149.
17. See Allen Wood's discussion of this point in *Kant's Moral Religion* (Cornell Univ. Press, 1970), pp. 13-34.

dom and happiness, and "religion is the recognition of all duties as divine commands."[18]

A moral purpose is evident even in the limitations to human knowledge, Kant asserts. If we had fuller knowledge of God, we would be driven by fear and not out of duty, and this would contradict our freedom and be counterproductive to moral development. God wisely allows us only conjectures about nature rather than clear proofs, because only when respect for duty supersedes desires and fears are we allowed a view of the supersensuous world.[19]

But the scope of moral teleology becomes even more evident in the *Critique of Judgment*. There Kant points out that if the purposes proposed by the moral law are at least possible, human freedom is intended to influence the natural course of events. For moral actions are performed in the empirical world and affect events there; the empirical world *is* the world of nature, and we tend to think of nature as being affected by our actions. But why? What ground can there be for such a harmony of the unknown bases of natural phenomena with human freedom? Kant draws attention to a factor omitted from his previous two *Critiques*. Both had dealt with the faculties of understanding and willing; mediating between these two is a third faculty, the one that becomes engaged in aesthetic experience. Kant goes on, then, to explore aesthetic judgments about both art and nature, showing that they, too, imply a teleology.

In aesthetic judgment, the form of the object harmonizes with *a priori* cognitive structures to produce pleasure; this suggests a purposiveness in the way an aesthetic object appeals to human reflection and in the way a human being experiences the object. We also find ourselves describing natural processes in terms of purpose, for particular empirical laws are not isolated phenomena but are interconnected in an astounding overall network that bespeaks intelligent purpose. Natural processes interweave for the sustenance of animal life, and the natural order somehow conspires to provide all the conditions for life and freedom that are necessary to human society. Our judgments in such cases are plainly teleological, even

18. *Practical Reason,* p. 134. J. Stout (*The Flight from Authority,* p. 234) calls the autonomous "moral point of view" an invention attempting to overcome the crisis of authority.

19. *Practical Reason,* p. 153.

though the concept of purpose is not empirically based. It is instead the precondition of our judgments.

Kant debates whether this purpose is merely phenomenal, an ideal we bring to nature, or objectively real. Hobbes had modeled his account of human beings and society on the mechanistic laws of physics, but Kant thinks it absurd that a second Newton could explain living things in accordance with laws devoid of rational intention. The amazingly beautiful forms we find in the natural kingdom speak loudly for the reality of "the aesthetical purposiveness of nature."[20] Although the idea of purpose is indeed a regulative principle in human thought, it is derived from the concept of freedom rather than from the categories of theoretical thought. On the one hand, if it is an ideal only, then nature's processes are either mechanistically determined as Democritus supposed (this is impossible) or a necessary emanation of Being in some fatalistic Spinozan sense (and this is itself another indemonstrable idea). On the other hand, if the purposiveness of nature is real, then either natural life is itself end-oriented (as in primitive hylozoism), or else it derives from an intelligent and purposive Being, and theism is true. Kant opts for the latter.

The question then arises as to God's purpose in making nature thus, and here again an overall moral teleology is revealed. An initial hint comes from the similarities between aesthetic and moral judgment. The contemplation of nature's beautiful forms, apart from the alluring charm of its empirical qualities, requires a frame of mind analogous to disinterested moral thinking apart from the allurements of sensory pleasure. Beauty is like moral goodness: it harmonizes with *a priori* concepts of the understanding; it claims universal agreement; it requires disinterested reflection; it frees us from self-interest.[21]

The similarity suggests that nature's overall purpose is human moral development. Nature is not self-serving, for the vegetable kingdom serves the animal kingdom, and the vegetable and animal kingdoms serve human happiness and culture. But in doing so they contribute to the disciplining of the moral will. The purpose of nature, as Richard Kroner sums it up, becomes clear:

20. *Critique of Judgment,* trans. J. H. Bernard (Hafner, 1951), p. 193.
21. *Critique of Judgment,* pp. 140-45, 196-200.

When Kant conceives of nature as a phenomenal realm, his intention is not so much psychological (and not even epistemological) as ethical; nature is phenomenal because it is nothing but material for the moral will. Nature is phenomenal . . . because man as a moral person is never permitted to derive his ultimate ends from nature; on the contrary, he is required to subject nature to his own ultimate ends. Nature is phenomenal because it is destitute of ultimate ends and of an absolute meaning: both end and meaning are finally connected with the moral will which uses nature as a means and thereby superimposes the realm of freedom upon nature.[22]

Kant's later historical writings make the same claim for history. He traces the emergence of reason from pre-rational instinct (interpreting Adam's expulsion from Eden to mean departure from an uncultured animal life to a state of reason) and suggests that we were impelled in this direction by our mutual antagonism in the original state of nature. Human history as a whole can be seen as the realization of Nature's secret plan, and the natural "end of all things" symbolized by the Day of Judgment is that consequences commensurate with one's virtue continue after this life in the noumenal world.[23]

This overall moral teleology in nature and history leads once again to postulating a moral deity as its author, and to a religion that recognizes "our duties as divine commands."[24] This is what Kant calls a "reflective judgment," not a logical conclusion, but it is nonetheless a matter of conviction.

Now, if this proposition, based on an inevitably necessary maxim of our judgment, is completely satisfactory from every *human* point of view for both speculative and practical use of our reason, I should like to know what we lose by not being able to prove it as also valid for higher beings, from objective grounds (which unfortunately are

22. *Practical Reason*, pp. 106-8. Cf. *Critique of Judgment*, pp. 279-98.

23. See especially "Idea for a Universal History from a Cosmopolitan Point of View," "Conjectural Beginning of Human History," and "The End of All Things," in Immanuel Kant, *On History*, ed. L. W. Beck (Bobbs-Merrill, 1963). Cp. *Anthropology from a Pragmatic Point of View*, trans. M. J. Gregor (Martinus Nijhoff, 1974), where he provides an empirical description of the natural cognitive and affective powers that bear on the moral life: the raw material that the will must rule.

24. *Critique of Judgment*, p. 334.

beyond our faculties). . . . So much only is sure, that if we are to judge according to what is permitted to us by our own nature (the conditions and limitations of our reason), we can place at the basis of the possibility of these natural purposes nothing else than an Intelligent Being.[25]

Kant's critical epistemology led to his rejection of natural theology, but his ethic leads to what he calls "ethico-theology." While some indications of what this involves appear in all three *Critiques,* the fuller development comes in *Religion Within the Limits of Reason Alone.* Kant begins with the evil in human nature. He rejects the overly optimistic Enlightenment claim that human nature has a predisposition for steady moral improvement: "it has certainly not been deduced from experience; the history of all times cries loudly against it."[26] But he also rejects the overly pessimistic view that, ever since the fall, humankind has increasingly gone from bad to worse. Instead he offers a middle position, based on the insistence that people are morally good or bad by virtue of the maxims governing their actions.

Three predispositions in human nature are distinguished: a disposition to animality, as a living being with needs and inclinations; to humanity, as a rational being able to exercise prudence in regard to those needs and inclinations; and to personality, as a moral being aware of obligation and accountability before the moral law. While all three are dispositions to what is good, they still admit the possibility of evil, whether by the frailty of human nature (Kant cites the inner conflict the apostle speaks of in Romans 7), or its impurity in harboring other incentives than duty alone, or the wickedness of reversing the moral order and obeying inclinations rather than moral law. The problem in each case is in the exercise of the human will — its frailty in observing the moral maxims one has willed, or its impurity in confusing incentives of duty with those of inclination, or its perversity in deliberately neglecting duty.[27]

It follows that moral progress requires discipline of the inclina-

25. *Critique of Judgment,* pp. 247-49.

26. *Religion,* p. 15.

27. *Religion,* pp. 21-27. John Silber criticizes Kant's claim that the rational will cannot reject moral law since it depends on it. Kant therefore failed to see the radical nature of sin as rebellion and the possibility of a Nietzschean ethic. See Silber's introduction to Kant's *Religion* book, pp. cxxix-cxxxi.

tions, not only out of concern for health, reputation, or other benefits, but also by repeatedly willing the duty-maxim in faith that the moral ideal can be attained. This faith is a moral disposition towards the highest good, and God reckons it to us as righteousness.

In all of this Kant has in mind the Christian doctrines of sin and forgiveness, and of God as creator, lawgiver, and judge. Evil is not due to inclinations as such, for desires and needs can be God-given. Evil rather begins in the will, which must be converted to God, but human freedom remains such that I must choose for myself; no other being can do it for me. The doctrine of the Incarnation tells us that a moral archetype has come from heaven and assumed our humanity. The faith in this Son of God that makes us acceptable to God is an inner moral disposition to "be loyal unswervingly to the archetype of humanity" and remain true to this exemplar.[28]

Neither God nor other persons can ever make a person righteous, but we still benefit from a society aimed solely at the maintenance of morality. Such an ethical commonwealth (Kant calls it the "Kingdom of God") differs from a political one in that its laws are noncoercive. His essay *Perpetual Peace* envisions such a League of Nations. His comments on education reflect the same ideal; the young in particular need moral guidance, but they must constantly be urged to purity of moral motive. More influential than all the allurements of pleasure will be the attractiveness of pure virtue; stories of virtuous people and discussions of particular virtues will inspire love and respect for moral law. For moral culture must be based not on punishments but on maxims that train the mind to think.[29]

The title of Kant's *Religion* book is significant. He is limiting himself to "reason alone," that is to say, to the religious beliefs suggested by the preconditions of our moral consciousness. Historical religions, he believes, appropriately represent moral duties as divine commands. The Bible sets moral faith in the form of a narrative that imaginatively symbolizes the supersensible world. Kant interprets those symbols to mean that the supersensible is noumenal and a rational moral deity is objectively real.[30] If Kant detracted from historic Christian orthodoxy

28. *Religion*, p. 55.
29. *Practical Reason*, pp. 155-57. See also his *Education*, trans. A. Churton (Univ. of Michigan Press, 1960).
30. *Religion*, pp. 73-78 and bk. 4.

and contributed to the rejection of its historicity, it is because he interprets the biblical narrative entirely from the standpoint of his moral theory regardless of the authors' intentions.

In contrast to earlier "scientific" approaches, however, he grounds moral value not in social contract or utility, nor just in reason, but in what he believes to be reality itself. Not all subsequent Kantian ethicists have done this,[31] nor do they place the moral imperative in a larger teleological context. Yet Kant's view of the autonomy of will leads to an atomistic individualism in which each of us is in principle morally self-sufficient, and neither God nor other persons can do more than provide inspiring moral examples. Duty is reduced to a rational principle devoid of social or historical context. In the next chapter we shall look at this criticism as voiced by Hegel, a criticism that leads to the contextualizing of duty and in due course to an ethical relativism that denies both teleology and moral law.

31. I think of Alan Gewirth's *Reason and Morality* (Univ. of Chicago Press, 1978). Alan Donagan's *Theory of Morality,* however, was tied in his later thinking to Christian theology.

CHAPTER ELEVEN

Hegel: Idealist Ethics

HEGEL WAS ATTRACTED in his early years to Kant. With many of his contemporaries, he saw Kant's first *Critique* not as destroying metaphysics but as opening the way to a new metaphysic based on morality, such as the *Critique of Practical Reason* proposed. Kant's *Religion* book, moreover, saw Jesus as a moral reformer, a picture Hegel endorsed in an early essay on "The Spirit of Christianity and Its Fate": Jesus moved from oppressive commandments, without any freedom for individual judgment, to the idea of disinterested love for one's fellow members in the Christian community. What troubled Hegel and his circle was the phenomenal/noumenal dualism. They wanted to recover the metaphysical use of natural science, and relate it to morality within their philosophical vision of the moral universe as a whole.[1]

This early ambition contains the seeds of Hegel's more mature thought: the historical development of freedom, its societal nature, the role of reason, and the unfolding self-realization of Absolute Spirit. But it also gives birth to a persistent criticism of what he views as empty abstractions in Kant: the autonomy of an individual whose reason is isolated from desire, the remoteness of any moral world order as an achievable moral ideal, and the emptying of duty of any particular

---

1. On these biographical matters and the relationship of Hegel's ethic generally to Kant, see W. Kaufmann, *Hegel: A Reinterpretation* (Anchor Books, 1966); W. H. Walsh, *Hegelian Ethics* (Macmillan, 1969); and H. B. Acton's introduction to Hegel's early *Natural Law*, trans. T. M. Knox (Univ. of Pennsylvania Press, 1975).

content. Kant gives us abstract individuals with freedom in the abstract, reason in the abstract, morality in the abstract. This kind of abstract *Moralität* must be transcended. F. H. Bradley goes so far as to say that Kant's ethical system was "annihilated" by Hegel.[2]

Kant had been impressed by Rousseau's discovery of the self with its inner freedom and the corresponding notion of a social contract that expresses the general will. This atomistic picture of individuals had been evident in Hobbes and Locke, of course, and Kant never quite gets beyond it. The idea of individual freedom dominated his thinking; it inspired his emphasis on goodwill as the only thing of intrinsic value, and on autonomy as against any heteronomy of the will. We ought, in moral matters, to be quite independent of the world around us. But, Hegel objects, the solitary individual and the notion of acting out of duty alone are unreal abstractions. Self-consciousness itself is only possible in relation to some "other." It is, among other features, a state of desire affirming itself by taking things for itself. It has needs and wants that cry for satisfaction: it gains an identity by acquiring property; it finds satisfaction in a family. Individual self-realization apart from community is not really possible.[3]

By the same token a sense of duty alone is not moral consciousness. Duty for the autonomous will requires keeping alert to desires that might mislead. But desires also include the needs and wants that tie us to nature and other people. Kant's idea of a purely rational moral consciousness is thus incomplete; it divides up the individual self into reason and inclinations. Of course he acknowledges the opposition between duty and the desire for happiness, and postulates an eventual harmony in some remote future life. Reason demands it. But here, according to Hegel, Kant finds himself in a contradiction. On the one hand, to accept the desire for happiness as part of one's moral consciousness would destroy the exclusiveness of acting out of duty alone. On the other hand, reason must include the desire for happiness in thinking about the ideal, the perfect good. What really connects duty and our natural desire for happiness, Hegel concludes, is concrete action here and now. It is concrete actions, not ideal abstractions, that bring

2. F. H. Bradley, *Ethical Studies* (first published 1876; Bobbs-Merrill, 1951), p. 87 n.

3. See Hegel, *Phenomenology of Mind*, trans. J. B. Baillie, 2nd ed. (Macmillan, 1949), pp. 225, 469, *passim*.

duty into relation with the objects we need to achieve harmonious and satisfying identity.[4]

> Social ethics is the peak of the objective mind. Both the legal person and the moral subject function within it and are abstractions from it; they function within concrete finite objectively organized wholes. . . . The good will matures, however, by participating in such social wholes.[5]

If Kant recognizes this in the role he gives to a moral society, or in his distinction between the formal and material principles of moral choice, then he must grant that the formal principle of acting out of duty alone is indeed a misleading abstraction.

F. H. Bradley, the British neo-Hegelian, echoes his mentor's concern about harmonious self-fulfillment, extending his criticism to utilitarianism as well as Kant. Because it extends moral consideration to others, but reduces happiness to a collection of particular feelings, "its heart is in the right place, but the brain is wanting."

> Happiness for the ordinary man means neither a pleasure, nor a number of pleasures. It means the finding of himself or the satisfaction of himself as a whole . . . the self to be realized is not exclusive of other selves, but on the contrary is determined, characterized, made what it is by relation to others.[6]

Moreover, Hegel believes, Kant's abstract moral individual is so morally divided that no particular content of moral law can emerge. The categorical imperative required that the maxim for one's action could, without self-contradiction, be a universal law. This makes the moral criterion a form devoid of content and in effect a mere tautology: "Don't think what cannot be thought, don't will the unwillable!" But such indifference to content could accept any content as readily as its opposite, provided only that neither implies any self-contradiction. Ought there to be property, or not? "Property per se does not contradict itself. . . . Absence of property, absence of ownership of things, or again,

---

4. *Phenomenology*, pp. 615-21.
5. Hegel, *Encyclopedia of Philosophy*, trans. G. E. Mueller (Philosophical Library, 1959), §430, pp. 244-46.
6. *Ethical Studies*, pp. 38-40, 56.

community of goods, contradicts itself just as little."[7] So what difference does it make? Yet in actuality property arises out of need or desire, not out of moral reason alone. It has no value as an abstraction, but only in being mine or yours, related to our concrete identity.

> The absence of property contains in itself just as little contradiction as the non-existence of this or that nation, family, &c., or the death of the whole human race. But if it is already established on other grounds and presupposed that property and human life are to exist and be respected, then indeed it is a contradiction to commit theft or murder; a contradiction must be a contradiction of something.[8]

Kant's ethic, then, is too abstract; like his *Religion* book, it is an ethic "within the limits of reason alone."

Hegel finds a more concrete picture in the Greeks, where family and the civil society are microcosms of an overall moral order. Repeatedly he refers to Sophocles' *Antigone* and her appeal to the spirit of everlasting moral laws implicit in family devotion.[9] When she sees her brother as the embodiment of their family, and her duty towards him as the highest, this is not abstract, formal reasoning but the spirit of her natural emotion. Her love for her parents and brother sees them as members one of another. Their identity is inseparably one, and her brother an extension of herself. Family is a natural ethical community.

Similarly with economic community:

> The labor of the individual for his own wants is just as much a satisfaction of those of others as of himself, and the satisfaction of his own he attains only by the labor of others. . . .[10]

This is simply an empirical fact, and the reality of thus existing for others finds expression in customs and positive laws more concrete than either natural law or Kant's fruitless appeal to the law of noncontradiction. Kant's formalist ethic may have been a necessary stage in the unfolding

---

7. *Phenomenology*, p. 447.

8. Hegel's *Philosophy of Right*, trans. T. M. Knox (Oxford Univ. Press, 1967), §135, p. 90.

9. *Phenomenology*, pp. 452, 477, 491, 494-96; *Philosophy of Right*, pp. 114-15. See above, in Chapter 1.

10. *Phenomenology*, p. 377.

consciousness of human freedom, but the opposition between reason and natural feelings still had to be bridged. Reason shows itself most fully in the driving spirit of its laws, in passion for and loyalty to a cause.

This is an important change from the Enlightenment view of reason and the human person. The rule of reason no longer stands in opposition to the emotions, but rather finds fulfillment through them. The self is no longer defined in opposition to the objective world of mechanistic science, but as self-realizing spirit. A new understanding of freedom results, not the negative notion of freedom from the deterministic processes of nature or from our need for other persons, but the more positive notion of finding self-identity in relation to others.[11] Hegel's ethic is a social ethic, an account of actual historical situations *(Sittlichkeit)*, not an abstract set of rational principles *(Moralität)*, and he accordingly presents it by describing the historical realization of the idea of self-conscious freedom in what Walter Kaufmann pictures as "a pageant of living forms."[12]

Just as Antigone finds new freedom in loyal identification with her brother, so the individual family finds identity in a civic community. For freedom comes with undivided identity, and identity is only completely unified when it is self-sufficient. The family is self-sufficient in ways no isolated individual can be, and the civic body more so. But it, too, is dependent on outside sources to meet its needs and ensure its security. Only the nation-state can be fully self-sufficient, have undivided identity, and be fully free. A state is the macrocosm of which the local community, the family, and the individual are but smaller microcosms. It therefore commands the loyalty of its citizens, as the family claims the loyalty of its own. Our highest moral duty is then to the laws of the state. Again Hegel appeals to the Greeks:

> In a free nation, therefore, reason is in truth realized. It is a present living spirit, where the individual finds his destiny, *i.e.,* his universal and particular nature, expressed and given to him. . . . The wisest men of antiquity for that reason declared that wisdom and virtue consist in living in accordance with the customs of one's own nation.[13]

11. See Charles Taylor, *Hegel* (Cambridge Univ. Press, 1975), ch. 1.
12. Taylor, *Hegel,* p. 31.
13. *Phenomenology,* p. 378.

"When virtue," he says, "displays itself solely as the individual's simple conformity with the duties of the station to which he belongs, it is rectitude" — a line that gave Bradley the title for his famous essay, "My Station and Its Duties."[14]

Underlying both Hegel's criticism of Kant and the development of his own social ethic is his conviction that the basic task of philosophy is to overcome the conflict of opposites and reconcile them in a new harmony. He had watched the French revolution that started in his student days, and saw it complete a process of liberation that began with the Reformation — a process that led beyond both despotism and mob rule to a rational rule of laws. He shared the pre-Socratics' interest in how nature's processes exhibit a conflict of opposing qualities and forces, and he read history in that light. His *Phenomenology of Mind* describes in serial form varieties of human experience characteristic of intellectual history, showing how the insufficiencies of one worldview bring it into conflict with another, only to find reconciliation in a higher synthesis. Partial error is a necessary step towards truth as a whole.

Thus Kant is not altogether wrong. But reason and passion needed reconciling, and by doing that Hegel transcends the dichotomy of morality and science and of noumena and phenomena; for as reason acts by means of passion, so spirit is at work in nature and in the history of ideas and in history as a whole. Even his own *Sittlichkeit* is not the last word, for in the end ethics is incomplete, too, and gives way to religion.

But to claim that reason works through passion and that spirit is at work in history implies that all such processes are in some sense logical. Hegel describes their logic as a dialectic: as opposites conflict, a new harmony emerges, only to encounter new conflicts and find further reconciliation. Every thesis has a possible antithesis, but because they are only partial truths they can be harmonized in a larger synthesis. Opposition is not irreconcilable. Aristotle qualified his law of noncontradiction by saying that A cannot be non-A "at the same time and in the same respect," for it is an abstraction applicable only to abstract ideas independent of any concrete historical process. Dialectic is the logic of history; it describes the way in which ideas evolve in finite thought and in finite actions.

14. *Philosophy of Right*, p. 107.

One key example is the idea of an "individual" at which we have been looking. Kant's moral ideal is an abstraction, one isolated particular among others. It stands in opposition to the abstract universal, the concept of humanness as an ideal form never fully exemplified in any concrete case. But transcending this historic opposition between universal and particular is the individual as a "concrete universal," with both "universal *and* particular nature." The universal nature and particular characteristics interpenetrate, in that all members of a nation (or family, etc.) have things in common, a common identity above and within all their particular differences.[15] The nation is not just a collection of different individuals united only by force or social contract (or in the case of the family by biological and economic accident), but is rather one body united by history and by practical loyalties. The common will is not a blank tablet to be inscribed either by a despot or by popular vote, but is a common commitment to a unifying cause. The spirit of a nation is more real and more powerful than any abstract ideals or theories.

Hegel's view entails a doctrine of internal as against external relations. Individuals are not like atoms, mutually independent entities, related to each other only by the accident of causal influences extraneous to their inner nature — as in the case of Descartes's mind/body interaction. They are organically interrelated in such a way that the inner nature of each is different by virtue of their being together. The personalities and beliefs, the rights and duties, are different for everyone; yet the differences themselves are rooted in a mutuality of relationships. This account plainly fits marriage and the family, and Hegel extends it to the nation.

Yet even the nation and its *Sittlichkeit* is not the last word; it is not the Absolute. For while historical teleology draws us to fuller and fuller self-conscious freedom in the emergence of the nation-state, the Reason and Will pulsating throughout history is an all-inclusive Absolute Spirit — the Divine Logos itself.

Echoing the Platonic tradition, Hegel sees the goal of history as

---

15. See Hegel, *Encyclopedia*, §122-23; *Science of Logic*, trans. W. H. Johnston and L. G. Struthers (Allen & Unwin, 1929), vol. 2, pp. 234-57. Also B. Bosanquet, *The Principle of Individuality and Value* (Macmillan, 1912), ch. 11; F. H. Bradley, "My Station and Its Duties," in *Ethical Studies*, pp. 98-147; and A. J. M. Milne, *The Social Philosophy of English Idealism* (Allen & Unwin, 1962).

the realization of an archetypal Idea that is superior to that of any one individual or community, yet which lives and acts in each and all of us now, in the continuous process of human beings becoming conscious of their oneness and thus conscious of their freedom. The history of ideas is the history of this Idea, and the history of nations is the process of its increasingly concrete embodiment. The mind and will of a family or nation, its spirit, is enlivened and formed by its "independent self-consciousness united with its concept." This is what gives it ethical substance and finds expression in its art, religion, and philosophy; for its self-concept is a microcosm of the Idea of the whole.[16]

But we can take the parallel one step further: the Idea is in the mind of God. As a nation's self-concept has being only in an actual mind or spirit (the American Mind, the German Spirit, etc.), so too the Idea of the whole has being only in Absolute Mind or Spirit. The unfolding history of the Idea must therefore be seen as the unfolding self-consciousness of Absolute Spirit. The Absolute is a Self in which all the dialectic stages that time separates in the course of history are eternally present together. In history, the Absolute appears as what it is timelessly, conscious of itself. Individual morality, family devotion, and national loyalty are but concrete ethical expressions of belief in the Eternal.[17] Ethics once again culminates in religion.

Hegel has been criticized for subordinating individual freedom to the totalitarian demands of a state whose spirit is strengthened and unified by the conflict of opposites. War is not only glorified, it is made necessary. Indeed, the philosophical basis of Italian Fascism was provided by the neo-Hegelianism of Giovanni Gentile.[18] But if we grant Hegel that the Idea unfolding in history is the unified self-consciousness of Absolute Spirit, then the individualistic freedoms of the eighteenth century necessarily give way to national unification and independence movements in the nineteenth century and totalitarianism in the twentieth.

16. *Philosophy of Right,* §§156f., p. 110.

17. This is the basis on which Josiah Royce, the American idealist, built *The Philosophy of Loyalty* (first published 1908; Macmillan, 1924). Cp. his *Lectures on Modern Idealism* (Yale Univ. Press, 1919), lecture 6.

18. Taylor, *Hegel,* p. 45. See also M. Westphal, *History and Truth in Hegel's "Phenomenology"* (Humanities, 1979), ch. 7; and James Collins, *The Emergence of Philosophy of Religion* (Yale Univ. Press, 1967), chs. 6-8.

Hegel is also faulted for opening the door to ethical relativism. Even the *Sittlichkeit* of a nation-state is not the absolute, unchanging, final word about ethics. And F. H. Bradley explicitly declares that there are no fixed, absolute moral rules for all persons without distinction of times and places. Yet he hesitates:

> Morality is relative, but is nonetheless real. At every stage there is the solid fact of a world so far moralized.[19]

We cannot take our morality, then, from the moral world we find ourselves in. It is still evolving, and not the Ideal; it lacks the self-consistent unity that will eventually be. Improvement and social reform are still needed.

But Hegel's point is twofold. First, his account is descriptive, not normative, a historical narrative whose overall logic points the direction that events will be taking. Second, the nation-state is the highest *objective* manifestation of Absolute Spirit, but still stands in dialectical opposition to the struggles *subjective* spirit experiences between what necessarily is and what ought to be, given the creative possibilities still available. Subjective spirit is the realm of imagination, passion, and individual choices that affirm life and "the infinite value of every individual."[20] This opposition of objective and subjective spirit, like all the other dichotomies Hegel faced, has to be overcome. They find reconciliation in the more unified ideals of the art, religion, and philosophy where the Absolute is most fully manifest. There are thus higher loyalties than political ones: loyalty to beauty (in art), to good (in religion), and to truth (in philosophy); all of them for their own sake.[21]

Ethics culminates in religion. Were this not so, if Hegel's *Sittlichkeit* had no divine Absolute for its *telos,* then he would be nothing but a historical relativist. But in religion as in ethics, Hegel's point of departure is the work of Kant, and he follows Kant in interpreting religion from the standpoint of ethics. Ethics and religion both see the eternal working in history to realize the ideal, both are motivated by the need for reconciliation, and both lead to a union with the Absolute in which the opposition of good and evil is overcome and all are united

---

19. *Ethical Studies,* p. 125.
20. *Encyclopedia,* §§388-98, pp. 227-34.
21. See W. H. Walsh, *Hegelian Ethics,* ch. 2.

in love. The difference between them is that ethics depends on reason while religion appeals to feeling and the imagination, and this difference shows itself most in Hegel's insistence that theological beliefs are not literally true but symbolic. Art expresses the self-consciousness of the Absolute pictorially *(Bild)*, and while more primitive religions literalize images, more mature religions use symbols *(Vorstellung)* to represent the universal Idea. Philosophy, however, expounds that Idea as a concept *(Begriff)* underlying them all. Christian symbols are the most developed religious expression of the Idea, for its doctrine of creation finds the origin of everything in Eternal Spirit. God as Father represents the Idea itself; God the Son, the Logos, represents the Idea in historical consciousness and thought; and the Holy Spirit symbolizes the Idea at work in the concrete life of communities, the Kingdom of God on Earth. The Incarnation, then, tells us that the Absolute manifests itself in the finite so that everything finite is a particular embodiment of the Infinite.

Hegel's is not the God of Christian theology, but a spirit who lives only through the creative processes of history. The result is an immanentistic theology that makes creation necessary for the self-conscious existence of God. He transcends creation by his all-inclusiveness, instead of by the self-sufficient independence asserted by *ex nihilo* creation. Hegel consequently is unable to maintain any ultimate distinction between good and evil, for both are necessary to God. This is a problem native to monistic metaphysics from Neoplatonism onward, where every conflict must eventually be reconciled in an all-inclusive One.

Hegel's influence on nineteenth-century liberal theology and more recent process theology is plain. Indeed, Whitehead pays homage to F. H. Bradley in the preface of his *Process and Reality*. Whitehead's God, too, is the great harmonizer, dependent on nature for his self-realization. Apart from the creative processes of nature, the primordial nature of God consists only of "eternal objects," the Idea of every possible historical harmonization. It is an account of God, in Hegel's words, "as he is in his eternal essence before the creation of nature and any future spirit."[22] For Whitehead as for Hegel, only the consequent nature of God, realized by experiencing what transpires in creation, has concrete existence. Like Hegel's Absolute, he is dependent on nature, himself in process of being created. Whitehead is not the

22. *Science of Logic,* I.60.

monistic Idealist that Hegel was, but his dependence on Hegelianism produces the same kind of finite God and immanentistic theology in place of traditional Christian doctrine. He too sees conflicting opposites — good and evil, truth and error — all harmonized in the growing unity of God's experience.[23]

Metaphysical monism has had perennial problems in making room for both individual freedom and an ultimate opposition of good and evil. The American personal idealist, Edgar Sheffield Brightman, writes:

> If error and evil are wholly overcome in the Absolute, then they do not exist in the Absolute as they do in me, the human person. In me, error is really taken to be truth, and evil is really chosen instead of good. What there is in me cannot possibly be in the Absolute as I experience it. My ignorance cannot mean the Absolute is ignorant. And since all of my life is to some extent imperfect, none of my personality can be in God as a part of him.[24]

There is an "ineradicable logical contradiction" between what error and evil are for me and what they are for God.

Moreover, according to Brightman, the metaphysical oneness of finite persons with the Absolute makes both communion and cooperation with God meaningless, and so absolute idealism destroys the motive and meaning of religious experience.[25]

Brightman defines his own alternative as a pluralistic version of idealism:

> the belief that the universe is a *society* of conscious beings, that the energy which physicists describe is God's will in action, and that there is no unconscious or impersonal being. Everything that is, is a conscious mind or some phase or aspect of a conscious mind. To

---

23. See A. F. Holmes, "Why God Cannot Act," in *Process Theology*, ed. R. Nash (Baker, 1987), pp. 177-95; and "Ethical Monotheism and the White-headian Ethic," *Faith and Philosophy* 7 (1990): 281-90. Bradley did not elevate God to identity with the Absolute; Whitehead similarly does not equate God with the principle of Creativity that pervades nature, but God himself undergoes the creative process. See *Process and Reality* (Macmillan, 1929), pt. 5, ch. 2.

24. E. S. Brightman, *Person and Reality* (Ronald Press, 1958), p. 298.

25. Brightman, *Person and Reality*, p. 299.

speak religiously, the universe consists of God and his family. Nature is divine experience.[26]

Nature, then, has no causal power, no fixed laws of it own, no independent existence. But every natural event has meaning and value for God and is "the best instrument thus far forged to help persons grow." Fact and value are inseparably one in the reality of the divine experience.[27]

Now plainly a plurality of finite persons distinct from God provides more individual identity and freedom than one all-inclusive Mind; it allows for religious experience and an objectivity of values rooted in God. But the problem of evil persists. Brightman talks of "multiple meaning." Physical events are not good or bad except as they express or influence personality, for they only have meaning or value for persons; but the same event can have different meanings for different persons. To God, every physical event "means law and love," while to humans it may mean "lawlessness and hate." But God's loving purpose works constantly and patiently for the achievement of human good.

This kind of optimism is severely challenged by radical evils like genocide, poverty, and environmental destruction, not to mention calamities of nature such as hurricanes, earthquakes, and floods. Brightman speaks of "surd evil" for which no rational explanation seems possible, and a "given" factor in nature (the divine experience) that God did not create and over which he has no control. This "given" includes the laws of logic and Platonic ideas, plus nonrational elements in sensory experience and psychological impulses like desires, pleasures, and pains — in fact, the very ingredients that non-idealists regard as ineradicable facts. The difference is that for idealists like Brightman they are not produced by real natural causes, either in the external world or in our own bodies, but are simply the givens of all possible experience, human or divine. Some things we experience therefore have no specific purpose, no particular value for us or perhaps even for God. Surd evil can never be called good. The evolutionary process produces a vast amount of waste. But the overall process, we are told, makes it worthwhile.[28]

26. E. S. Brightman, *Nature and Values* (Abingdon-Cokesbury, 1945), p. 114. Italics are mine.

27. Brightman, *Person and Reality*, p. 297.

28. Brightman, *Person and Reality*, ch. 12; *A Philosophy of Religion* (Prentice-Hall, 1940), chs. 8, 9, and 10.

God, then, is finite in power even though his loving goodness is infinite. As an idealist, Brightman is locked into this conclusion. By denying the independent reality of natural forces and processes, he is left with no causal locus for natural evil except the intrinsic nature of experience in God himself and in the finite minds he created. A finite God needs the cooperation of his creatures in the endless process of overcoming evil for good. He cannot prevail alone. Brightman's pluralistic idealism, like Hegel's monistic idealism, offers a teleology devoid of the assurance that evil can ultimately be overcome by good. The oneness of fact and value remains incomplete.

CHAPTER TWELVE

Ethics as Empirical Science

In ethics, the influence of mechanistic science persisted with increasing intensity throughout the nineteenth and twentieth centuries. Premised on the rejection of any inherent teleology and the resultant dominance of efficient causes in moral psychology that we observed in the seventeenth and eighteenth centuries, it grew into a deliberate project of making ethics itself an empirical science. The French positivist Auguste Comte launched the project:

> After having instituted a vast mechanical hypothesis . . . [Descartes] finally subordinated to it the study of the chief physical functions of the animal organism. But when he arrived at the functions of the affections and the intellect, he stopped abruptly and expressly constituted from them a special study, as an appurtenance of the metaphysico-theological philosophy.[1]

Comte wanted to extend mechanistic explanations to intellectual and moral phenomena, in accordance with his empirical generalization about intellectual history that each branch of human knowledge passes successively through three different stages: the theological, the metaphysical, and the scientific. The first supposed that all phenomena are caused by supernatural beings; the second appealed to abstract forces and principles; the third studied the laws of causes and consequences

1. *The Positive Philosophy of Auguste Comte,* trans. H. Martinean (London, 1953), vol. 1, quoted from Patrick Gardiner, ed., *Nineteenth Century Philosophy* (Free Press, 1969), p. 151.

144

by observing invariable sequences of phenomena, without speculating about unobservable forces or metaphysical principles behind them. The time had come, he believed, when science could in this way extend its rule to the study of human behavior. He looked for causes that could be controlled — not inner causes like moral feelings or human purposes and beliefs but rather external causes that could be ascertained by behavioral studies, biology, or phrenology (the predecessor of brain science).

Comte was particularly concerned to apply this scientific approach to the problems of society, and his work represents the beginning of sociology as an empirical science. Jeremy Bentham, too, was socially and politically oriented, a radical in fact who questioned the acceptability of existing institutions such as the monarchy and the established church, on the grounds that they mainly serve the self-interest of the ruling class. His hopes, like Comte's, depended on science. The age of discovery and improvement in the natural world needed matching by similar discoveries and improvements in the moral world. The fictitious nature of social contract theory had already been exposed by David Hume. If we could now discover general laws of cause and effect that govern human behavior, major social improvements would be possible. According to Bentham,

> Nature has placed mankind under the guidance of two sovereign masters, pain and pleasure. It is for them alone to point out what we ought to do, as well as to determine what we shall do. On the one hand, the standard of right and wrong, on the other the chain of causes and effects are fastened to their throne. They govern us in all we do, in all we say, in all we think.[2]

With this general law of psychological hedonism, Bentham proposed ways in which pleasure and pain, whether physically, societally, or religiously caused, could be used. His proposals for penal reform were based on the utility of punishment in changing behaviors: by ensuring a sufficient surplus of pain over pleasure, we can predictably secure the desired effects. To this end he proposed to quantify pains and pleasures: their intensity, duration, certainty, immediacy, fecundity, and purity, as

---

2. Jeremy Bentham, *Introduction to the Principles of Morality and Legislation* (1823 ed.; Oxford Univ. Press, 1907), p. 1.

well as the number of persons involved. Here was a scientific basis for a penal system, and for legislation and policy decisions that could change people and society for the better.

The natural order, based on a psychological egoism in which individual desires and aversions rule, now becomes something to be changed rather than followed. Human nature is morally neutral, malleable stuff waiting to be molded to the requirements of universal happiness.[3] This was Bentham's scientific project: the shaping of behavior and of society for the maximum happiness of the maximum number.

John Stuart Mill was initially enthusiastic about Bentham's project. Tutored at home by his psychologist father, James Mill, a friend and colleague of Bentham, he found that Bentham's utility principle "gave unity to my conception of things" and that it took on the role of a religion in giving purpose to his life.[4] At the age of 20, though, he suffered an emotional crisis involving severe depressions, in which he realized that the achievement of all his utilitarian dreams could not really make him happy. Something was badly missing that cold science could not supply. He turned to poetry. Bentham regarded poetry as useful if it gave pleasure, but nonetheless as a misrepresentation of life. Not so Mill. Reading Wordsworth for the first time showed him the need to cultivate feelings as well as analytic thinking. From Coleridge he learned the importance of imagination, for Coleridge added to mechanistic explanations an "organic imagination" that grasps the organic unity of living, growing things.[5]

Increasingly Mill saw what was missing. He complained that Comte gave no place to inner causes of human conduct, as against those accessible to biology, behavioral observation, and "phrenology."[6] Bentham had too thin, too superficial a view of human nature and happiness, with nothing to say about the feelings or the person as a whole, nothing about social feelings, nor about a conscience distinct from self-interest or outward acts of benevolence, nor about one's sense of honor and love of beauty, nor about order and action, nor indeed

---

3. See Charles Taylor, *Sources of the Self* (Harvard Univ. Press, 1989), p. 320.

4. *Autobiography of John Stuart Mill* (Columbia Univ. Press, 1944), p. 47.

5. P. H. Abrams, *The Mirror and the Lamp* (Oxford Univ. Press, 1953), pp. 167-77. See also J. S. Mill, *On Bentham and Coleridge* (Harper & Row, 1950).

6. See J. S. Mill, *Auguste Comte and Positivism* (Univ. of Michigan Press, 1961), p. 8.

our love of loving itself, of family life and human intimacy in general. This inner life, including virtue and the life of the mind, yields pleasures qualitatively higher than the external pleasures Bentham had considered, and it is this inner life as a whole that is distinctively human.

> It is better to be a human being dissatisfied than a pig satisfied; better to be Socrates dissatisfied than a fool satisfied.[7]

Yet Mill remained convinced that human nature is so constituted as to desire only what is part of or a means to happiness. The promotion of happiness remains the test for all our rules of conduct. We will not achieve happiness by making it the immediate goal of our actions, but indirectly by concentrating on the particular ends of what we do. For if happiness is a state of the person as an organic whole, and virtue is part of happiness, we must cultivate virtue and all that comprises the inner character necessary to happiness as a whole.

But is this emphasis on the inner life still empirical science? Mill included chapters on the moral sciences in his writings on logic.[8] Ethics combines the methods of art and science; as art, it defines the end to be attained, while as science it investigates causes and conditions so as to propose rules and policies that will lead to that end. It is art, not science, that affirms holistic happiness as the end, although the means to that end are the business of moral science. Laws of the formation of character, for example, are not deduced from the end, but from more general laws of human behavior, although they are confirmable by observation.

General laws are inductive generalizations, but Mill was dissatisfied with then-current views of induction as a simple enumeration of instances without any formal logical connection to generalized conclusions. He argued first that all generalizations logically depend on the uniformity of nature, which is neither an article of *a priori* knowledge

---

7. J. S. Mill, *Utilitarianism* (Bobbs-Merrill, 1957), p. 14. On these qualitative differences among pleasures, see pp. 12-20; see also Mill's essay on Bentham in *On Bentham and Coleridge* (Harper & Row, 1950), pp. 66-98.

8. J. S. Mill, *A System of Logic* (Harper, 1860), chs. 11-12. At the end of ch. 12 he explicitly admits that the cultivation of noble character should be an end to which the pursuit of happiness (except as it is included in his idea of character) gives way. But, he continues, happiness decides what constitutes the elevation of character.

nor something known intuitively, but is itself an empirical generalization of the broadest scope. So all knowledge is basically empirical, even mathematics; Euclidean geometry rests not on intuitive axioms but on postulated definitions or empirical hypotheses. Second, he argued that general laws about social phenomena are not deduced, as had been thought, from laws of history, for laws of history are themselves just broad generalizations that presuppose laws about social phenomena. He therefore developed inductive methods designed to provide believable general laws, and in doing so helped introduce the hypothetico-deductive view that dominated philosophy of science into the second half of the twentieth century.

Mill, therefore, had to explore the causes not only of overt human behavior but also of the inner feelings that Bentham ignored. And this poses difficulties, for the inner life is more obscure, more complex, with multiple causes that cannot all be reduced to one efficient cause, as Bentham assumed. The general laws that govern the inner life may describe major causal influences, but they cannot take into account the less evident minor causes that can upset our predictions. No one motive is absolute, as Bentham had supposed. Moral science will then be approximate, without the predictable certainties of sciences like astronomy — or Bentham's hedonic calculus.

James Mill had developed an influential analysis of the mind as a complex of passive sensations combined by uniform psychological laws of association.[9] He assumed, however, that the order of our sensations was ultimately derived from the order of objects in the natural world. His son, John Stuart Mill, was not convinced. Relationships between sensations are not empirically given but must be investigated. We experience a structureless world of atomized sensations and feelings that, on investigation, are found to be related in various ways due to psychological principles of association.

Moral feelings in particular are neither innate, as moral sense philosophy implies, nor basic givens, but are derived from other feelings. Consider the sense of duty, which is the essence of conscience. It is a complex phenomenon derived by association from sympathy, love or fear, desire for approbation, or religious feelings. Similarly, our social feelings arise from mentally associating ourselves with others, so that

9. A helpful account of eighteenth-century analytic methods is in J. H. Randall, *The Career of Philosophy* (Columbia Univ. Press, 1965), bk. 6, ch. 7.

we come, as though instinctively, to regard the good of others as naturally as we regard our own good. These inner feelings are the ultimate psychological sanction in the moral life.[10]

But what of social order? If there is no natural order to human experience and none we know of in the external world, but only the associations we build, must not the same apply to the social order? Bentham had attacked the natural law theory with which Sir William Blackstone had defended the legal and penal status quo. He had discarded the idea of a natural community as fictitious, and for him the common good is nothing but the sum of individuals' goods that legislation harmonizes for maximal benefit.[11] For Mill, social stability like individual morality rests on the inner sanction of our social feelings, and so is due to the acquired habit of subordinating individualistic impulses to social ends (the task of education), to a feeling of loyalty to something lofty with which we identify by association, and most strongly to a feeling of common interest and oneness with others.[12]

These inner sanctions produce social justice and preserve liberty, independently of traditional theories. Bentham had rejected natural rights on empirical grounds: not all people actually possess them, and if they did, anarchy would predictably result.[13] Mill rejected them, as he did any social contract, as needless abstractions, for justice and liberty are simply names we give to certain social utilities that stand higher on the scale than some others. No metaphysical theory and no theological appeal are needed; Mill's utilitarianism supports justice and liberty with his underlying moral psychology.[14]

But does not Mill's psychology itself make metaphysical assumptions? Ethics as empirical science depends on a knowledge of the causes and consequences of human behavior. But Mill locates the most important causes in the inner self, with its own self-cultivation. He himself asks the key question:

---

10. J. S. Mill, *Utilitarianism*, ch. 3.

11. Bentham, *Principles of Morality and Legislation*, ch. 1. See also Alasdair MacIntyre, *A Short History of Ethics* (Macmillan, 1966), pp. 232-35.

12. J. S. Mill, *On Bentham and Coleridge*, pp. 124-26.

13. Jeremy Bentham, "Anarchical Rights," reprinted in *Human Rights*, ed. A. I. Melden (Wadsworth, 1970), pp. 28-39.

14. *Utilitarianism*, ch. 5, and *On Liberty*, ch. 4.

Are actions of men, like all other natural events, subject to causal laws? Does that constancy of causation which is the foundation of every scientific theory . . . really obtain among them?[15]

He grants that the science of human nature is not an exact science, like astronomy, and that it has more predictive power for political bodies than individuals, but he still insists that "ethology" (moral science) develops empirical laws that can be explained causally as in the natural sciences. So his question remains: are human actions really subject to causal laws? Are they causally determined?

This depends, of course, on what we mean by causation, and here Mill follows Hume. Empirically we only observe sequences of events, not causal forces connecting them. Mill's sensationalism is again at work here, for the idea of causal connection is only an association that rides piggyback on repeatedly contiguous sensations. Mill makes a crucial distinction: empirical laws describe but causal laws explain.

He explicitly rejects the view that acts of will are uncaused. Rather, he insists that, given empirical laws describing human conduct, if we knew a person's character, motives, and desires we could unerringly predict how he will inevitably act. But this does not mean the person can do nothing to change his ways. In opposition to both Bentham and his own father, he insisted that inner character is something we ourselves can change. "Self culture" is his constant theme:

Though our character is formed by circumstances, our own desires can do much to shape those circumstances. The utility of the doctrine of freedom is the conviction that we have real power over the formation of our own character; by modifying circumstances we can modify our future habits or capabilities of willing.[16]

Our desires are determined by the joint influence of motives and individual character. If our character is such as to cause us to do wrong, we can, if we desire improvement, cultivate motives that will make us strive for improvement and so emancipate ourselves from the inevitability of doing wrong.[17] Since the stronger motive prevails, the educa-

---

15. *Logic*, p. 521.
16. J. S. Mill, *Autobiography*, p. 119.
17. J. S. Mill, *An Examination of Sir William Hamilton's Philosophy* (New York, 1877), vol. 2, p. 299.

tion of our feelings as to what will really maximize happiness assumes for Mill major importance.

This sounds as if he finds human freedom and causal determinism logically compatible. He regards freedom not as indeterministic, un-caused action, but as a self-determinism, with complex inner causes rather than external ones in which I play no part. The "feeling of freedom" is unaffected by knowing these causes are at work. The term "feeling" is important, however, for it flags an empirical point of ref-erence. Mill draws on Hume's distinction between constant conjunc-tions — the observable contiguities that govern our association of ideas — and necessary connections. This distinction, he complains, is missed by both fatalists and indeterminists, the one affirming causal necessities we cannot prove scientifically and the other claiming that uncaused acts of will contradict necessitarian claims. The solution is to drop the term "necessity" altogether, since it has no empirical basis. Free acts may, then, be caused but, because of the multiplicity of major and minor causes, not be predictable. The question remains, however, as to whether the "feeling of freedom" is all that is at stake in causal deter-minism. It is the major point of appeal for indeterminists, but the debate is about more than the feeling. And while Mill holds back from metaphysical commitments, he does seem to think that real causal connections govern all of nature, including our inner life.

Yet he adopts a phenomenalist position, saying that George Berke-ley's discoveries deserve "a permanent place among positive truths": the subjectivity of primary qualities such as externality, distance, and mag-nitude; the nominalist rejection of abstract ideas; and the needlessness of any material substratum.[18] All we know directly is our own ideas, and the patterns our minds produce. Mill puts these discoveries to use in his critique of Sir William Hamilton's Scottish Realism, arguing that belief in an external material world is not intuitive at all, but results rather from psychological laws of association that cause us to take repeatedly similar sense experiences to reveal some permanent material substratum. The word "matter" does not signify such an abstract idea at all, but simply arises from the psychologically induced expectation of "the permanent possibility of sensations." Belief in the existence of "matter" is not amenable to proof.

18. "Berkeley's Life and Writings," in Mill's *Three Essays on Religion* (AMS Press, 1970), p. 263.

Thus, then, as body is the unsentient cause to which we are naturally prompted to refer a certain portion of our feelings, so mind may be described as the sentient subject of all feelings. . . . But of the nature of either body or mind, further than the feelings which the former excites, we do not, according to the best existing doctrine, know anything.[19]

"Substance," when used of either matter or mind, is merely a general term for the possibility of experience. For empirical science, then, neither mind nor body has any permanent existence or identity. All we know in this regard is the flux and pattern of our own sensations and feelings, and all we have sufficient evidence to believe is the permanent possibility of further sensations and feelings.

This phenomenalist conclusion has obvious implications regarding belief in immortality. What is the verdict of science on a separate soul? We have no proof that it is the organization of a body that does or does not cause consciousness, for "brain" stands for nothing but a set of actual or possible sensations that observers of the "brain" might experience. The conscious states we call "mind" might occur under other conditions, for all we know. Science provides no proof either way.[20]

"Nature" is to be understood as just a collective term for all phenomena, actual or possible, that do or could occur without voluntary human intervention. So when Mill speaks of the uniformity of nature and of laws of nature, he presumably refers just to uniform phenomena rather than the underlying realities. Yet he takes causal laws so seriously and as so basic to everything else as to suggest that they represent more than just constant conjunctions. As Copleston points out, he slides into ontological assumptions.[21] But if, perchance, human unpredictabilities are due not just to multiple causes but also to uncaused initiatives, the whole project of a scientific ethic is ill-conceived.

Phenomenalism, in fact, is an unstable position. Imposing the methods of natural science on the study of human nature and conduct

19. *Logic*, 1, ch. 3, sec. 8. See also *Examination of Hamilton's Philosophy*, chs. 11, 12, and 17.

20. See "Immortality" and "Theism," in Mill's *Three Essays on Religion*, pp. 197-211.

21. F. Copleston, *A History of Philosophy* (St. Martin's Press, 1950), vol. 8, p. 86.

confines us to what natural science can catch. So Bentham and Mill slide towards a naturalistic view of persons, a slide that twentieth-century philosophy of mind has made increasingly explicit. Coleridge saw the pretensions of mechanistic science as a threat: "a useful working hypothesis in physical research illicitly converted first into fact, and then into a total world view."[22] Mill tried to qualify it with emphasis on a causally active inner life; but belief in free self-culture has a reverse tendency away from naturalism and towards either idealism (as with some Romantics) or some kind of mind/body dualism. For the scientific approach alone fails to explain the creativity, complexity, and power of the self and its inner life.

Mill resisted all metaphysical dogmatism: not only fatalistic necessitarianism and substance theories of matter and mind, but also such theories in religion. Bentham was an atheist, but not Mill:

> Positivism need not deny the supernatural, only throw it back to the origin of things. What caused nature to be?[23]

He shows none of the reverence for nature and the natural order that we find in Enlightenment deism. If nature's universal laws kill, torture, and ruin people, then conformity to nature has no connection with right and wrong, despite what natural law ethics claims. If moral science legitimately improves human nature, why should moral law follow nature unchanged? The duty of humans is the same in both respects: not to follow but to amend it. We can only learn what good Providence intends "by considering what tends to promote the general good, and not what man has a natural inclination to," for inclinations may be fetters that impede that good.[24]

Mill rejects the supposed perfection of both the natural order and any conceivable divine being. Only one supernatural belief seemed clear of "intellectual contradiction and moral obliquity," namely Manichean dualism, for nature looks like the product of a struggle between good and evil.[25] But religion must be treated as a strictly scientific question,

---

22. M. H. Abrams, *The Mirror and the Lamp*, p. 310. Likewise Anthony Quinton: "Classic utilitarianism is a secular and naturalistic doctrine" (*Utilitarian Ethics* [St. Martin's Press, 1973], p. 15).
23. *Auguste Comte and Positivism*, p. 14.
24. *Three Essays on Religion*, p. 55.
25. *Three Essays on Religion*, p. 116.

testing its claims by the same methods as science applies to all other subjects; unified scientific laws may point to monotheism, but how strong is the evidence?

The cosmological argument illegitimately argues back to a first uncaused cause. Science knows only causes and effects in regular sequences; ultimate beginnings are beyond science. The argument for design is on better ground, for induction can appeal to numerous cases of design for an end. Seeing and hearing, for example, result from the structuring of eye and ear as if by some intelligent being. Probably, then, God contrived means to ends, carefully adapting them to conditions independent of his will. This, however, is no reason to suppose any ultimate beginning of the matter or forces to which nature must adapt its processes. All that it shows is the wisdom and limited power of a benevolent being who desires the pleasure of his creatures' pleasure, namely a finite God.[26]

While belief must be proportioned to the scientific evidence, religion may still be morally useful even if it is not intellectually demonstrable. In the early stages of history, belief in the supernatural elevated moral ideals for society and provided motives for doing what is right. In an age of science, society no longer needs supernaturalism either to tell us what is right and wrong in social morality, or for supplying motives. But religion still addresses the imagination, and like poetry it supplies ideals "grander and more beautiful than we see realized in the prose of human life."[27] It is a source of personal satisfaction, of feeling for love and beauty, and of hope with regard to both the government of the universe and life after death. It makes life feel far greater, adds solemnity to social feelings, and encourages the improvement of one's character.

But is it reasonable? In utilitarian terms, yes. The analogy to Mill's own experience is clear. What he himself found in the poetry of Wordsworth and Coleridge, he realizes others find in religion. Both poetry and religion involve the imagination. In a letter to Thomas Carlyle written in his twenties, Mill stated he had been reading the New Testament: "properly I can never be said to have read it before."[28] He

---

26. See "Theism," in *Three Essays on Religion,* pp. 167-95.

27. "Utility of Religion," in *Three Essays,* pp. 100-105.

28. Cited by Karl Britton, *John Stuart Mill,* 2nd ed. (Dover Publications, 1969), p. 214.

expressed unbounded reverence for Jesus as a moral teacher and leader, and for the ideals he represented. Enlarging on this at the end of *Theism,* his last major writing, he points out that, regardless of historical criticism, the Jesus of the Gospels fills the moral imagination even of unbelievers, translating abstract ideals into a concrete goal, "so to live that Christ would approve our life."[29] While Mill finds this well suited to Comte's "religion of humanity," the fact is that the life and teachings of Christ go far beyond a scientific approach to ethics. Who Christ was, the question of his deity, is one that the positivist stage of human thought leaves behind. Yet while scientific method cannot address such a theological question, Mill acknowledges that the moral quality of Jesus' life and teaching has not only social utility but unparalleled beauty and grandeur.

In effect, then, Mill outgrew the superficial reductionism of Bentham's view of persons, of happiness, and of moral character because he was drawn beyond an exclusive dependence on what science can describe and explain. Unable to remain consistently a phenomenalist, unable to settle for Bentham's reductionism, he found some kind of theism more compatible with his ethic of the inner life.

The record of subsequent attempts to develop an ethic on the model of empirical science confirms its inadequacy. In terms of the present discussion, though, its shortcomings may be summed up as follows:

1. *Empirical science cannot define the good,* says Mill, but can only propose what means would best contribute to such an end. Phenomenalism affords no basis because it cannot establish the unity of the self, as Henry Sidgwick later noted:

> Grant that the Ego is merely a system of coherent phenomena, that the permanent identical "I" is not a fact but a fiction, as Hume and his followers maintain; why, then, should one part of the series of feelings into which the Ego is resolved be concerned with another part of the same series, any more than with any other series?[30]

Sidgwick himself appealed to intuition rather than empirical generalization. But, while we intuitively recognize certain experiences to be

29. *Three Essays,* p. 255.
30. Henry Sidgwick, *The Methods of Ethics,* 7th ed. (Hackett, 1981), p. 419.

good, G. E. Moore denied that we can thereby define "good."[31] A definition is an analytic statement that, since the subject and predicate terms are logically identical, is necessarily true. But this is plainly not the case with the hedonist definition, "the good is pleasure," for it can be contradicted. The same is true of any attempt to define the good by reference to either empirical or metaphysical facts: they all commit the "naturalistic fallacy" of equating natural with nonnatural properties. If we accept the empiricist distinction between analytic and factual statements, then the good remains indefinable.

It was a small step from this to positivism's emotivist theory. If moral judgments are neither analytic statements defining ethical terms, nor empirically verifiable statements of fact, then — again assuming the empiricist acceptance of only these two kinds of statement — moral judgments are not meaningful statements at all. They are simply emotional outbursts, perhaps calculated to influence others' behavior.[32] Ethics as empirical science had run into a dead-end street.

2. *Empirical science cannot ground moral duty.* Mill's scientific approach limited him to discussing the *sense* of duty in relation to other feelings with which it was causally associated, including the influence of religion. He could not relate these feelings to anything objectively real — for instance, to some natural law in a providentially ordered world — because his phenomenalism kept him from asserting theological or metaphysical beliefs. Only psychological or perhaps sociological grounds for the sense of duty were available.

A similar picture continues in later empiricist ethics. Some, like Moore, attempted to derive the "right" from the "good," but for the positivist both kinds of language reduced to emotive expressions. Post-positivists found that "ordinary" or natural language had a "prescriptive" function in ethics,[33] but this empirical analysis of how language functions is analogous to Mill's analysis of moral feelings: a psychological or sociological ground, not a basis for objectively real duty. The resurgence of normative ethics that followed the demise of logical positivism turned to a contractarian basis for duty, most notably in John Rawls's *Theory of Justice;* but the social contract — as Bentham

---

31. See G. E. Moore, *Principia Ethica* (Cambridge Univ. Press, 1903), ch. 1.

32. The best-known expression of this is A. J. Ayer, *Language, Truth, and Logic* (Dover Publications, 1946), ch. 6.

33. See R. M. Hare, *The Language of Morals* (Oxford Univ. Press, 1964).

observed — is from the empiricist standpoint a fiction, like Plato's "likely story." Yet where else can the empiricist turn to provide an objective basis for moral duty?

Stephen Toulmin observed decades ago that we reach "limiting questions" where psychological and linguistic answers give way to metaphysical and theological ones. About the same time Elizabeth Anscombe aptly remarked that for half a century the concept of moral law had been excluded from ethics. How, she asked, can such concepts as moral law and duty survive without a lawgiver?[34] She was referring, of course, to natural moral law, and since that remark an increasing literature has emerged on both natural law and other versions of divine command ethics (for which more will be said in our final chapter). Since empirical science could not ground moral duty, metaphysical and religious grounds return.

3. *Empirical science cannot support human hopes.* Mill is quite explicit that belief must rest on evidence, and there is insufficient evidence in religious matters to establish more than the existence of a finite god — not that God brought matter into existence, not that he providentially governs nature and secures his purpose, and certainly not that he became flesh and dwelt among us. Yet Mill allows that hope in such a finite, unknowable God is logically possible based on imagination, not evidence. Belief rests on evidence and so is scientifically supported, but hope rests on imagination (as does art), regardless of its lack of scientific support. If the Jesus of the Gospels captures the imagination, people may logically hope that he is more than human, but the belief itself is groundless.

It was this kind of attitude that William James addressed in his famous 1896 lecture, "The Will to Believe."[35] If an option between two rival hypotheses is "live" rather than irrelevant, forced rather than avoidable, and momentous rather than trivial, and yet the evidence on each side carries equal weight, we can properly choose which to believe on passional rather than evidential grounds. James's point is that the

---

34. See S. E. Toulmin, *An Examination of the Place of Reason in Ethics* (Cambridge Univ. Press, 1958), pts. 3 and 4; E. Anscombe, "Modern Moral Philosophy," *Philosophy* 33 (1958): 1-19.

35. Published in William James, *Essays in Pragmatism* (Hafner, 1948). James probably had in mind W. K. Clifford's essay, "The Ethics of Belief," in *Lectures and Essays* (Macmillan, 1879), which took an evidentialist approach essentially like Mill's.

demand for sufficient evidence is both unreasonable in some of life's circumstances, and presupposes a one-dimensional view of the person as an intellect for whom feelings and desires are irrelevant. If Mill then wants to do justice to the feelings and the entire inner life, he too should be open to other than evidentially based beliefs. If imagination does not necessarily misrepresent things, as Bentham had claimed of art, then Mill should at least grant that some of what it presents may well be true. Supernaturalism itself may well be true, for all that stands in its path is naturalistic leanings that make everything we experience subject to uniform laws of nature — itself a passional commitment that underlies Mill's entire philosophical project.

In conclusion, then: ethics as empirical science begins by reducing persons to inherently unordered complexes of sensations in need of scientific manipulation and management. Mill sees the one-dimensionality in this account and tries to change it, but his phenomenalism permits no metaphysical theory about human nature to limit the scientific takeover or make room for imagination's (and religion's) richer view of the self as an organic whole. And this phenomenalist account of persons is too thin to sustain an adequate ethic or to ground Mill's own values.

Utilitarianism is not the only attempt to make ethics an empirical science: John Dewey's instrumentalism is another.[36] There Hegel's *Sittlichkeit* reappears in Dewey's notion of a problem situation that challenges our emotional equilibrium and puts something we desire at stake. Ethics becomes scientific problem-solving; we come up with hypotheses for resolving the problem and test them experimentally before putting them into operation. Dewey accepts Comte's thesis of the methodological unity of the sciences and plainly wants to free them from theology and metaphysics. Equally plainly, though, his view of persons also is too thin to sustain more than a situational approach. In Dewey's view, human problem situations are part of the evolutionary adjustment process; natural selection proceeds in our case through the capacity of human intelligence to draw on its fund of experience in developing instrumentally valuable ideas. Questions about a highest good are therefore ill-conceived, for human nature is subject to change like everything else. There is neither unchanging natural order nor divine purpose to which appeal can be made, and no ground for the hopes religion stirs

36. E.g., John Dewey, *Reconstruction in Philosophy* (Henry Holt, 1920), ch. 7.

other than the intelligence humans have for resolving all their problems. Such was Dewey's evolutionary optimism.

Bertrand Russell's much-quoted pessimism may be more realistic. In "A Free Man's Worship," he draws a brief summary of "the world which science presents for our belief":

> That Man is the product of causes which had no prevision of the end they were achieving; that his origin, his growth, his hopes and fears, his loves and his beliefs, are but the outcome of accidental collocations of atoms; that no fire, no heroism, no intensity of ·thought and feeling, can preserve an individual life beyond the grave; that all the labors of the ages, all the devotion, all the inspiration, all the noonday brightness of human genius, are destined to extinction in the vast death of the solar system, and that the whole temple of Man's achievement must inevitably be buried beneath the debris of a universe in ruins. . . . Only within the scaffolding of these truths, only on the firm foundation of unyielding despair, can the soul's habitation henceforth be safely built.[37]

---

37. *Mysticism and Logic* (Anchor Books, 1957), p. 45. J. S. Mill, it should be noted, was Russell's godfather.

CHAPTER THIRTEEN

Nietzsche:
Fact and Value with No God

FOR WELL OVER two millennia, ethics was grounded in realities that transcend both historical change and human choice. It began with a cosmic justice reflected at the micro level in the ordered life of human individuals and then gave rise to teleological theories of universals in a theology of divine creation. Under the influence of nominalism, such appeals to cosmic order and purpose eventually gave way to a focus on the presumably unchanging aspects of the created person, as in Kant and the Scottish realists. Hume had disengaged these psychological foundations from theism, but still maintained a universalizable ethic. For Bentham and Mill, however, little unchangeable about human nature remained, apart from psychological hedonism and a causal malleability. But it is only with Friedrich Nietzsche that the relativizing process is completed. With no moral world order, no God, and no unchanging human nature common to all, no grounds remain for universal values apart from those of our own making. Nominalism had rejected metaphysical abstractions while retaining a world of particulars as the objective reference of language, but Nietzsche goes a huge step further. He rejects the notion of objective reference altogether, and thus rejects the representational function of language. Language is our own creation; and through language we create our values, our worlds, ourselves. Everything is a product of time.

We have arranged for ourselves a world in which we can live — by the postulating of bodies, lines, surfaces, causes and effects, motion and rest, form and content; without these articles of faith no one could manage to live at present! But for all that they are still unproved. Life is no argument; error might be among the conditions of life.[1]

The law of causality, he points out, may simply be "a very well acquired habit of belief, so much a part of us that not to believe in it would destroy the race." But it is not for that reason true.[2] The atomists' belief in "last remaining things that stay fast on earth" has similar status: a belief, a postulate; and as for so-called "substance," from the perspective of a living being it may be important to distinguish necessary from accidental properties and thereby affirm that enduring substances exist, but nothing real needs to correspond to such concepts. Nietzsche rejects not only the formal and final causes of Scholastic metaphysics but also the material substances and efficient causes of mechanistic science.

> Let us be on our guard against saying that there are laws in nature. There are only necessities: there is no one who commands, no one who obeys. . . . When you know there is no design, you know also there is no chance.[3]

Forms, species, laws, purposes are all equally undemonstrable. They stem from our compulsion to arrange a world for ourselves in which our existence is made possible, a compulsion thereby to control it.[4] But we know nothing of universal, inherent ends, or any other aspects of cosmic order.

Similar doubts extend to psychological concepts and beliefs. The psychological atomism of people like Hume and Mill is as ungrounded

---

1. F. Nietzsche, *Joyful Wisdom,* trans. Thomas Common (Macmillan, 1924), §121. Richard Schacht devotes ch. 3 to "Metaphysical Errors" in his systematic exposition, *Nietzsche* (Routledge & Kegan Paul, 1983). See also Joseph Simon, "Language and the Critique of Language in Nietzsche," in *Studies in Nietzsche and the Judaeo-Christian Tradition,* ed. J. C. O'Flaherty et al. (Univ. of North Carolina Press, 1985). Cp. Mill's view that we construct our "objective" worlds from atomistic data.

2. *The Will to Power,* trans. W. Kaufmann and R. J. Hollingdale (Random House, 1967), p. 273.

3. *Joyful Wisdom,* §109.

4. E.g., *Will to Power,* pp. 282, 355.

as physical atomism and the idea of an indivisible soul substance. "Soul" is only a word for something about the body, "reason" and "spirit" just toys of our bodily life. The "I" is something the body does, not a substance independent of it. To whom, then, do we assign the imagined raptures of being transported from our bodies and from this earth, when we experience a physical revulsion against the misery of sickness? To our bodies and this earth, of course; soul and immortality are meaningless fables we create in a degenerate search for some unchanging world of being.[5]

Free will is caught in the same net of suspicion; it is a lie aimed at controlling us by creating guilt, whereas in actuality we are necessarily what we are, pieces of fate devoid of purpose or meaning.[6] Will, like the "I," is a will o' the wisp; there are no "mental" causes.

Belief in God fares no better. Nietzsche chides Plato for inventing the Good-in-itself, declaring that metaphysics sprout from religions. Jewish priests too created their moral world-order by affirming that God willed, once and for all, what man is to do and not do, so that people are valued according to how much or little they obey. But this turns things upside down, for it makes a virtue of what is not a condition of life. Christianity does the same thing: in saying "yes" to another world, it says "no" to life; and in making a fictitious world the real world it makes what is "nothing" into "God."[7]

Nietzsche claims, then, that God is dead. This is more a historical verdict than a metaphysical one; the Judeo-Christian God has been exposed for the nothing he is, and his law is now unworthy of belief. A religion that says "no" to life is not itself a needful condition of life, and it has no life-function to keep it going. What is not a condition of life harms life, undermines its strength, debilitates it. It is no longer a live option.

Belief may have played a psychological role at earlier junctures of history, but Nietzsche sees neither theoretical nor pragmatic reasons for believing in God. Kant's moral argument cannot help, for he made a fictitious moral world order into the real world. The more traditional

---

5. *Thus Spake Zarathustra*, I, in *The Portable Nietzsche*, ed. W. Kaufmann (Viking, 1954), pp. 142-47. See also *Twilight of the Idols*, in *The Portable Nietzsche*, p. 484.

6. *Twilight of the Idols*, pp. 492-500.

7. *Beyond Good and Evil* and *Ecce Homo* (Henry Regnery, 1955), pp. xi-xii; *The Antichrist*, in *The Portable Nietzsche*, pp. 24-25; *Genealogy of Morals* (Vintage, 1969), III, §17.

arguments for God depend on metaphysical assumptions Nietzsche discredits. Similarly, he remains skeptical of all objective grounds for ethics in nature, in human psychology, and in God. "The whole of history," he says, "is the refutation by experiment of the principle of the so-called world order."[8]

This line of criticism is what he calls "experimental thinking." He is hypothesizing: "What if . . . ?" And he then extends the experiment by calling into question the value of truth itself. Immediate certainties, for instance, are far from being clear and distinct; Descartes's "I think" supposedly refers to an "I" that does the thinking and an activity the "I" supposedly causes, while assuming we know what thinking really is. But none of this is certain. Where do I get the concept "thinking"? Why suppose that an "I" is the cause, since a thought comes when *it* will, not when *I* will?[9]

Nor is logic itself immune from suspicion. It presupposes that things are ordered in such ways that reasoning is justified, yet the illusion of order is itself an after-effect of belief in God as creator. Logic assumes there are identical cases in order to generalize and draw inferences, but this stems from our will to generalize or infer, not from the demands of truth. Even the law of noncontradiction, that we cannot both affirm and deny one and the same thing, is an imperative we issue, not an independent logical necessity we merely recognize. It may control the realities we structure for ourselves, but not reality-in-itself. What, then, is truth but an invention for preserving oneself against others?

> . . . truths are illusions about which one has forgotten that this is what they are; metaphors which are worn out and without sensuous power.[10]

We say "God is truth," but God is nothing. We merely keep believing in truth so as to have something certain to hold onto, a crutch for the weak, like other metaphysical beliefs. And we treat it like a woman, making it sacrosanct, not to be violated.

Nietzsche's point is that behind language and logic and truth and their supposed sovereignty stand value judgments, stipulations due to

8. *Ecce Homo*, p. 328.
9. *Beyond Good and Evil*, §16.
10. "On Truth and Lie," in *The Portable Nietzsche*, p. 47. See also *Will to Power*, pp. 262, 277, and 279.

"physiological demands for preserving a certain type of life." The real question is not whether a belief is true but whether it furthers and maintains life, whether it preserves, cultivates, or trains a certain type of person. Philosophers treat truth with detached seriousness as an objective thing-in-itself, but that approach is as ineffectual in mastering truth as it would be in wooing a woman. English utilitarianism, with its scientific method, is a prime case. Its positivism is an "unnatural self-glorification of intellect." Kant's pure reason was fruitless because it is a kind of philosophical asceticism that castrates the intellect. Philosophers in general are "sly defenders of prejudices they christen 'truths,'" great philosophies the personal confessions of their originators, "a type of involuntary and unaware memoirs." All philosophy is merely perspective projected on a supposed world.[11]

Nietzsche is utterly relentless in his experiment. The son of a Lutheran pastor, he retained more than all else a dauntless passion for truth-seeking. When he challenges the claim that God is truth he is pursuing the truth about truth, for it is human knowledge-claims he most suspects. Morality, like all purported knowledge, is merely an interpretation, a symptom of something about the moralist. Instead of pursuing "moral facts," then, he pursues a natural history of morals. What is the truth about how morality arises?

His campaign against morality began, he says, in *The Dawn of Day*, where he declared morality to be nothing but obedience to customs that arose as useful ways of meeting needs or handling fears. Custom or tradition became a higher authority "not because it commands what is useful to us but merely because it commands," and this hinders the "formation of new and better morals; it stupefies." Our morality is then a kind of forgery from motives largely unknown, a human construct that Nietzsche deconstructs by uncovering hidden psychological roots. Custom applauds self-mastery, for example, not because it is useful to the individual — which is the exception — but because it shows the power of custom itself.[12]

Traditional ethical theories are given the same kind of psycho-

11. See *Beyond Good and Evil*, Preface and First Article; *Genealogy*, III, §12. Cp. John T. Wilcox, *Truth and Value in Nietzsche* (Univ. of Michigan Press, 1974), chs. 6 and 7.

12. *Ecce Homo*, p. 290; *Dawn of Day*, trans. J. M. Kennedy (Macmillan, 1924), §§9, 19; *Beyond Good and Evil*, §§75-77.

analysis. Stoicism adopts *apathia,* indifference to life's circumstances, as the natural good so as to make all of nature in its own rational image. Egalitarianism is a mask that hides a desire for equal power. Utilitarianism's benevolence towards the masses masks the condition of those too weak to assert themselves. Nietzsche's sarcasm is devastating:

> Hail you worthy molehill climbers,
> Ever "take-your-own-sweet-timers,"
> Growing stiff in head and knee,
> Soul of wash rag, face of poker,
> Overwhelming-mediocre,
> Sans génie et sans esprit![13]

His complaint throughout is about the "slave morality" of modern Europe. In whatever guise it appears, it calls "good" what benefits the weak and degenerate and calls "evil" what hurts them. Frustrated with life and unable to do anything about it, the slave achieves his revenge not by physical revolt but by subverting values. He gives his weaknesses flattering names — cowardice, hesitancy, powerlessness, and inoffensiveness become virtues like "patience" and "forgiveness" — and he gives his master's controlling strengths unflattering names like "injustice" and "cruelty." This act of "ressentiment," the seemingly self-denying power play of the weak, is what makes morality the hypocrisy it is and saps modernity of its creative virility.[14]

Nietzsche applies this psychological explanation to specifics. People find pleasure in feeling pity and showing compassion for those in need because it masks their own suffering while giving in to the suffering of others; in feeling sympathy, it engages in self-pity. Love for a neighbor is either veiled self-love, a self-indulgent weakness prompted by the bad instincts of sick natures, or else it is a power play that elevates me above those I help. The ascetic affirms his independence of the world, free from worries, compulsions, and disturbances, to make this life a bridge to another kind of existence. Finding pleasure in pain and self-sacrifice is "ressentiment" against life itself.

Nietzsche's overarching complaint about modern morality is that it says "no" to life, to nature. Pity subtly rebels against what nature does, asceticism against life itself. Moralities that propose to make people happy

---

13. *Beyond Good and Evil,* §228. Cp. §201.
14. On ressentiment see *Genealogy,* I, §§10, 13, and 14.

are rejecting life's realities. The three most lied about things, he suggests, are sex, the desire to rule, and self-love, which are in reality the most natural expressions of love for life there are; yet morality spiritualizes love for life by teaching self-control and self-denial. But life is cruel towards the weak and without pity for the dying; courage and conflict are natural and accomplish greater things than love of neighbor. Morality that says "no" to nature makes people smaller and smaller.[15]

One obvious example of this "no" is the pessimistic philosopher Schopenhauer's verdict that this is the worst of all possible worlds. Admired by Nietzsche as a young man, Schopenhauer viewed the physical world as a phenomenon projected by one's will, blindly and irrationally striving for what in reality is nothing. Since life affords more pain than pleasure, the only path is to deny the world and deny one's own will. Nietzsche soon saw the inconsistency, for Schopenhauer was a flautist who played his flute each day after dinner, and talked of harming no man.[16] What sort of nay-saying to life is it to preserve others from harm?

If nothing in life has meaning, no moral interpretation of the world can survive. Nihilism means that every ordered world we posit will fail; that every unchanging being is a deception, psychologically based and therefore nothing; that science has it all wrong; that both natural and economic order are anarchy; that history is blind fate.[17]

This nihilism, Nietzsche argues, is rooted in the Christian interpretation of human distress, for Christianity points us away from this fallen world to an eternal life where change and decay will no longer be seen. Otherworldliness is the greatest danger humanity faces. Christianity and Buddhism are religions for sufferers and defectives; they preserve what should by nature have perished, and so further the deterioration of the race.

> . . . to reverse every bit of love for the earth and things earthly and control of the earth into hatred of things earthly and of the earth: *this* was the self-assumed task of the church.[18]

Christianity began, then, as "ressentiment" against life, a popular uprising by underprivileged publicans and sinners, by the sick and

15. *Joyful Wisdom*, §26; *Zarathustra*, pp. 159, 281, 300; *Ecce Homo*, p. 268.
16. *Genealogy*, III, §6; *Beyond Good and Evil*, §186.
17. *Will to Power*, pp. 12-13, 44-45.
18. *Beyond Good and Evil*, §62; *Joyful Wisdom*, §143.

women, against their Jewish religion. Nietzsche approved the Old Testament's acceptance of suffering and death but saw the New Testament as moving in an opposite direction. Jesus' talk of paradise as he faced the cross was a sign of weakness. When his disciples projected a triumphant kingdom of God to come, they were merely voicing their ressentiment. Paul overcame his guilt before Jewish law by escaping to Christianity, then impudently taught the impossible — a resurrection of the dead. Luther restored the church just when it was vanquished, robbing Europe of Renaissance science's reaffirmation of the natural world.[19]

Christianity, then, corrupted humanity. It turned to God as a counter-concept to nature, invented a soul to degrade the body, and sin to degrade the passions. Sinfulness is not a fact of life but a misinterpretation of one's own depression, existing only in the consciousness of sin and guilt known as "conscience." Likewise, conscience is not the voice of God but of ressentiment only, an irrational self-punishment. The good then becomes a self-sacrificing love that identifies with life's failures — the weak and the poor, the sick and the slaves. Christian altruism is mass egoism of the weak.[20]

Nietzsche calls for a re-examination:

> One has taken the *value* of these "values" as given, as factual, as beyond all question . . . in supposing "the good man" to be of greater value than "the evil man," of greater value in the sense of furthering the advancement and prosperity of man in general. . . . But what if the reverse were true?[21]

The ideas of good and evil are worn out, benevolent intentions with disconcertingly disastrous consequences, and life has therefore lost its meaning. The advent of nihilism was necessary to make us rethink our values, but now that the morality of good and evil has run its course, the time has come to end the experiment and make a fresh start. We need to move "beyond good and evil" and ask what is really good or bad for the human race.

---

19. *Dawn of Day*, §68; *Genealogy*, I, §8; *Antichrist*, §§23, 41-43; *Will to Power*, pp. 108-10. On this topic see Karl Jaspers, *Nietzsche and Christianity* (Henry Regnery, 1961); and O'Flaherty, *Studies in Nietzsche*.

20. *Genealogy*, II, §20-22; III, §§16, 20; *Beyond Good and Evil*, §61; *Ecce Homo*, pp. 312-14, 332-34.

21. *Genealogy*, Preface, §6.

Nietzsche reiterates that we do not discover values and meanings that are already here, nor do they come to us from heaven; rather, we create them and give them to ourselves. *The* meaning, the way *for all,* does not exist; if God is dead, *we* must give meaning to the earth. We must will a good, an end to pursue, a strong and creative spirit, an *Übermensch.* All beings create something beyond themselves, a next stage in their historical development, and we must choose to be the surging edge of a tide that reaches beyond what humankind has yet been. "Let your will now say: the overman shall be the meaning of the earth!"[22]

This new breed says a passionate "yes" to nature, however tragic life may be. Life is so filled with creative possibilities that all its suffering is worthwhile. Nietzsche has in mind the heroic aristocratic virtues of ancient Greece and the Dionysian values that offset the calm rationality of an Apollo. Peace and order, even self-preservation, are not the good to choose, nor is happiness or equal rights; all of these represent the slave morality. The master morality by contrast pursues what is noble and distinguished: strength and honor; courage, beauty, and pride; a creative and selfish individualism that disregards the weak. Whatever heightens the feeling of power and nourishes this higher type is good; whatever is born of weakness is bad. The reversal is plain: not "no" to life but "yes," and a ready "yes" to the pain and suffering life brings.

Every morality manifests an underlying will to power, not just the master morality. Among slaves it is the will to freedom; among some who are stronger it is a will to equal rights with rulers, or a will to sacrifice themselves out of pity for others. Knowledge, too, is a tool of power, for without knowledge the human species could not live. Nietzsche comes up with a grand hypothesis: if thinking and morality are an interplay of life's drives and desires, if life with its desires evolved from the material world, and if we believe in the causal power of will, then nature itself is basically will to power. He adopts this hypothesis and applies it universally. Having rejected all metaphysical bases for ethical objectivity, he adopts a metaphysical basis of his own, a basis for rejecting ethical objectivity.[23]

22. *Zarasthustra,* Preface and p. 125. See also *Beyond Good and Evil,* §260; *Antichrist,* §2.

23. Walter Kaufmann notes three views of Nietzsche's *The Will to Power:* it is a crowning magnum opus; nothing new; and ideas not yet ready for publication. See editor's introduction to *Will to Power.*

Will to power, then, is a universal, unremitting drive, a creative force underlying the world process as a whole and in every part. Nietzsche emphasizes the time-process, history: it is as if our will and our values are drifting endlessly down the river of becoming, carried along by currents they cannot control, with no inherent aim. It is Heraclitus revisited, without a logos. It is Hegel's view of history unfolding, without a rational Absolute. Unlike Hegel's, the process has no consummation, no telos, but echoes the eternal cycles of Greek cosmology. Moreover, if time is infinite while force is finite, then the number of possible changes and combinations is finite and all possible states of affairs must have occurred earlier and will occur again. Whatever happens has happened before and will happen again. This is what we must live with, then: the realities of eternal recurrence. Ressentiment says "no" to it, and postulates another world where weakness is allowed. It takes a strong-willed master-morality to say "yes" to nature's wasting of the weak, to enduring the same pain and the same tragedy an infinite number of times, to using that pain and tragedy as a tool to nourish power, not grudgingly but with joy in the forebodings of uncertainty and delight in eternal recurrence.[24]

This universal will to power is clearly a naturalistic conception. "Over all things stand the heaven 'Accident,' the heaven 'Innocence,' the heaven 'Chance,' the heaven 'Prankishness.'"[25] It is an impersonal, irrational, unpredictable kind of force, an endless struggle among myriads of power-centers that results in changing relationships between those centers and changes in their very identity, a veritable chaos. Instead of a law-governed mechanistic universe, it is more energistic, more organic; akin to vitalism but without the substance-concepts. Life is not an entity but a dynamic process of conflict and change in a multiplicity of interrelated forces. Even power-centers — quanta of energy — are not a sufficient hypothesis without an encompassing intention, a will to power. Like a Dionysian orgy, life is an unrestrainably inexhaustible overflowing of creative force in which conflict and pain are stimuli to further creativity. This is the physiological basis for

---

24. *Will to Power*, pp. 544-50; *Zarasthustra*, pp. 435-37, etc. See also Ivan Soll, "Reflections on Recurrence," in Robert Solomon, ed., *Nietzsche* (Anchor Books, 1973), pp. 322-42.

25. *Zarathustra*, p. 278. See also *Will to Power*, pp. 331-41. Richard Schecht provides a helpful interpretation in his *Nietzsche*, ch. 4.

calling morality one human biological function among others. Virtues are refined physiological passions, beneficence a development of the sexual drive, justice a perfecting of the drive to revenge.[26]

This is a naturalistic evolutionary theory in which humankind can be seen as a bridge between the animals and what now looms on the horizon of the future, namely the *Übermensch,* the "overman." Evolution, however, is rather a struggle for power than for survival, because life is already profuse and can safely be squandered. Even where there is occasionally a fight for existence, Darwin was wrong; not the fittest but the weak often survive, simply because they are in the majority and show care, patience, self-control, and cunning — characteristics the strong despise. Moreover, a new organ cannot evolve because of its usefulness, because in its formative stages it has no use and so could not survive. The key evolutionary influence is not the external circumstances an organism must adapt to, but the inner drive to exploit those circumstances for the enhancement of its own power. That is why Christianity acts against the interests of the species: in moving selflessness and neighbor love to the fore and making all individuals of equal value, it denies the principle of selection (which is the will to power) and substitutes a mass egoism of the weak.[27]

Nietzsche's objection to Christian ethics and modern ethics is thus primarily cultural and historical, and he ascribes the same psychological roots to their theological and metaphysical bases as to ethics generally. His language is highly metaphorical, full of hyperbole and intentionally provocative. Not surprisingly he has been variously interpreted and variously influential: first as an advocate of the heroic virtues of aristocratic Greece, then as a precursor of the atheistic, existential struggle for meaning (note Sartre's Nietzschean "If God is dead, then anything is possible"), more recently as an early postmodern deconstructionist in hermeneutical theory, and still more recently as the major source of genealogical approaches to ethics.

Crucial to all of these interpretations is his perspectivalism: there are no bare facts, only interpreted facts reflecting different perspectives on life. Foundationalist epistemology was mistaken about universal truths from which philosophical conclusions can be logically derived

26. *Will to Power,* pp. 148-50.
27. *Will to Power,* pp. 141-42, 343-44, 362-63; *Twilight of the Idols,* pp. 522-23.

as a basis of ethics. Philosophers today recognize the validity of the complaint that we see through a glass darkly.[28] Nietzsche's "hermeneutic of suspicion" also has its merits. Merold Westphal calls him a "secular theologian of original sin" for exposing the self-deception of the human psyche.[29] But it does not follow that everything is totally relative, that different individual perspectives are *toto caelo* different, and that historical perspectives change one hundred percent. Sin has a universal, historically invariable nature, Westphal notes, that is manifested in localized historical ways. Likewise, any historical perspective on life reflects the same or similar aspects of human nature and human concern in a somewhat common world. Human perspectives have at least three dimensions: the generically human, the historical and cultural, and the idiosyncratically individual. (The generic alone would be quite skeletal, and is always fleshed out in different historical forms.) An individual's psychology is then not the whole story, nor is one's historical dependency. Nietzsche's own views, to whatever extent they may be correct, reflect the universal human condition in a common world, in a growingly post-Romanticist age, while also manifesting his own experiences and psychological condition.

Overgeneralization is, of course, a rhetorical strategy, if seemingly self-contradictory for one who rejects universal truth. Nietzsche talks as if there is really no such thing as truth, while relentlessly pursuing a generalized truth about why people imagine there is. He universalizes his psychological explanations of truth and morality as if they tell the whole story, falling headlong into the genetic fallacy of assuming that antecedent feelings are sufficient causes. He attacks morality as a whole, only to preach a higher one. He explores the will to power in others, and laughs at the rejoinder "Et tu, Brute!" It is a mocking rhetoric, making fun of logical and theoretic concerns. But he makes his perspectivist point more provocatively by virtue of his hyperbole.

Perspectivalism, however true it may be of human knowledge and interpretation, need not imply that there is no objective truth (how then could perspectivalism be true?) and no objective moral value. We must distinguish epistemological subjectivity and objectivity (i.e., to

---

28. The present author argued 30 years ago that all philosophy is "perspectival," in *Christian Philosophy in the Twentieth Century* (Craig, 1969).

29. Merold Westphal, *Suspicion and Faith* (Eerdmans, 1993), p. 230.

what extent knowledge is perspectival or not) from metaphysical subjectivity and objectivity (i.e., whether things exist and are what they are independently of our knowing them).[30] Nietzsche may be in measure correct about the epistemological subjectivity of the human situation, but it does not follow that no objective truth or goodness exists, only that we may not fully know it as it is in itself. Knowledge is indeed perspectival, and we owe thanks to Nietzsche for making us suspicious of foundationalist and other objectivist claims; but that does not deny the independent reality of the objects we think we know. Anti-realist that he is, he tends to equate our difficulty in knowing exactly what an object is in itself with a denial of the metaphysical fact that it exists — regardless of our knowledge of it, and regardless of our perspective or psychological history.

If Nietzsche's suspicions are overgeneralized half-truths and his genealogy of morals an interesting but overdrawn hypothesis, then it does not follow that truth and goodness are just illusions we create. Even on Nietzsche's terms, there are at least two different kinds of metaphysical hypotheses: traditional ones like Judeo-Christian theism that ground objective morality, and his own kind of evolutionary naturalism. A Nietzschean hermeneutic of suspicion could apply to both. And if the choice were reduced, as he says, to a question of pragmatic consequences, we would do well to recall Russell's warning about human hopes and aspirations being doomed to extinction in a naturalistic universe. The alternative perspective — belief in a Logos-ordered cosmos — grounds objective truth and goodness, gives purpose to life and viability to reason, and offers the hope of an eventually moral world.

30. On this distinction see A. F. Holmes, *All Truth Is God's Truth* (Eerdmans, 1977), chs. 1 and 3.

CHAPTER FOURTEEN

In Retrospect

THE PRECEDING ACCOUNT has briefly traced the historical roots of twentieth-century moral philosophy and attempted to show the close tie between the fact-value relationship and conceptions of God. It is time now to take stock of our findings, first of all by distinguishing the four general positions encountered.

The first approach, beginning in early Greece, grounds morality in the overall cosmic order. It continues in Plato's forms, Aristotle's teleology, and Stoic natural law; and it finds expression in the Logos theology of the Alexandrian and medieval church. Kant developed a more conceptualist version of this approach, in which natural phenomena contribute to moral development. Hegel further adapted this idea in his historical unfolding of freedom as the growing manifestation of Logos. The entire cosmic order is intrinsically teleological; this is the *maximalist position*.

A second approach limits itself to moral psychology. Aristotle's influence continues here, but not his teleology. Nominalism took its toll, along with the rise of mechanistic science. This approach is therefore a modern development, beginning with Descartes on the passions but more fully developed in regard to moral sentiments in eighteenth-century writers like Hutcheson, Hume, and Thomas Reid. While these psychological foundations of morals are attributed to the moral purposes of God, a mechanistic conception of nature prevails. Indeed, psychological factors are often themselves regarded as causal forces. Natural causal law is then the will of God. This moral psychology approach is thus a *mediating position*.

A third approach, emphasizing "the will of God and right reason," began with Ockham and the nominalists. What constitutes "right reason" varies; although it may draw on aspects of moral psychology, it tends to be consequentialist thinking. To the Ockhamist, God's will meant what Scripture commands; to Hobbes, it meant what the sovereign decrees. By the time we get to Mill, our rational powers are no longer ascribed to God at all; right reason is simply scientific thinking, Bentham's secularized application of mechanistic science. Any factual basis for moral values must be purely empirical: a hedonistic psychology and pleasurable (or painful) experiences. This is the *minimalist position*.

The fourth approach, Nietzsche's nihilism, is of course the most secularized, rejecting any fact-value relation at all. With no God and no natural moral order, we are left in a value-free world. Egoistical psychology never achieves the moral point of view, for reason masks power plays and God becomes a puppet manipulated by the church. To paraphrase Sartre, if God is dead and universals no longer exist, then anything is morally possible. "Right" and "wrong," "good" and "bad" have no objective reference, no basis in fact at all. This is the *moral sceptics' position*.

Nietzsche and other deconstructionists are not alone in this conclusion.[1] Others fail to see any basis for values in a world of causal determinism or of cultural and historical relativity. But Nietzsche speaks for them all. In a value-neutral world where God is dead and values have been historicized and psychoanalyzed to death, what basis for ethics remains other than one we create by the power some of us exert over others, or by the useful fiction of a social contract?

The obvious response is to deny Nietzsche's premise and reopen the fact-value question. Its long influence in several strands of philosophy, its ongoing fruitfulness, and its agility in the face of objections, all argue for its continued viability. Before proceeding, though, four key issues need to be identified:

1. The first and most obvious is the appeal of philosophers, even in the minimalist position, to *the will of God in regard to ethics*. Such an appeal today reverses the Enlightenment's rejection of authority and revelation and its commitment to "reason alone." Elizabeth Ans-

---

1. See, e.g., R. Rorty, *Contingency, Irony, and Solidarity* (Cambridge Univ. Press, 1989), pt. 1.

combe pointed out in a landmark article, "Modern Moral Philosophy," that moral law without a lawgiver could not survive the explosion of utilitarianism in the first half of the twentieth century. By mid-century, in the aftermath of the Nazi holocaust, divine command theories were therefore finding renewed acceptance, and more recent work by Robert Adams, Philip Quinn, and Richard Mouw has contributed significantly in refining and defending such an approach.[2] It speaks to the unchanging nature of the good and the ultimate source of moral obligation, while leaving open questions about moral knowledge. Since God's wise will lies behind cosmic order, moral psychology, and right reason, it is in principle compatible with either natural law theory or moral sense philosophy or with adaptations of Kantian or utilitarian approaches.

But the modern mind objects that authority of any kind violates the vaunted autonomy of individuals and contradicts Kant's fundamental principle about acting independently of external concerns out of respect for duty alone. Yet no one is an island. Hegel's criticism on this point is just. The individual devoid of desires and needs, independent of all social responsibility, is an unrealistic abstraction. To define self and duty independently of the webs of relations that give us our identity and pose our responsibilities is impossible. The Christian's sense of self is likewise tied to external relationships, hence to the community of faith and more basically to God. The sense of duty is bound up in this, too, so that the will of God becomes the natural and the logical point of reference in every regard. Moreover, if our identity is bound up with others whether we recognize it or not, then whether or not we recognize our dependence on the Creator, the will of God may still be the ultimate and universal basis of ethics. The Enlightenment conception of complete autonomy is simply mistaken.[3]

2. If we want to go beyond the minimalist position, however, we

---

2. See E. Anscombe, "Modern Moral Philosophy," *Philosophy* 33 (1958): 1-19; R. M. Adams, "Religious Ethics in a Pluralistic Society," in *Prospects for a Common Morality*, ed. G. Outha and J. Reeder (Princeton Univ. Press, 1993), pp. 93-113; Philip Quinn, *Divine Commands and Moral Requirements* (Clarendon, 1978); R. J. Mouw, *The God Who Commands* (Univ. of Notre Dame Press, 1990); Paul Helm, *Divine Commands and Morality* (Oxford Univ. Press, 1981).

3. See further Jeffrey Stout, *The Flight from Authority* (Univ. of Notre Dame Press, 1981).

also need to reopen the discussion of *teleology* that was aborted by the rise of mechanistic science. With no final causes inherent in natural processes but only matter and physical forces, nature became — as Tennyson put it — "blind" to the good. Hence the shift from cosmic order to moral psychology. But when Hume argued that our moral feelings give value to things, he saw no logical connection between the psychological "is" and any "ought," and he found nothing of value in itself. G. E. Moore's naturalistic fallacy follows — the fallacy of identifying the good either with some natural property like pleasure, or with some metaphysical property. If nature is morally neutral, then any attempt to ground ethics in a metaphysics of nature must fail.

But is nature morally neutral? William Frankena argued in 1939 that the naturalistic fallacy is not a fallacy at all if we add to the existence of natural properties a further premise about the value-laden status of such properties[4] — which is of course what not only Platonism but also appealing to the "will of God" does. At the risk of oversimplification, we might say that, while some fact F does not by itself logically entail value V, yet (F + V) does entail V. With divine command theories similarly: because God is altogether wise and good, what he commands is also wise and good. While, in the abstractions of pure logic, the bare fact of some natural property may not entail a value judgment, yet in concrete situations all facts have value-potential. We value art and science, virtue, peace, health, etc., in concrete situations for themselves as well as for other ends, but not just as abstractions. Neither in theistic perspective nor in concrete experience are facts value-free.

Recent developments in ethics make this plain. For all his rejection of a "God's-eye point of view" and his denial that theology and absolute ethics have reference to any real objects, Hilary Putnam rejects positivist claims that nature is an uncaring machine and argues persuasively for the mutual entanglement of fact and values in terms of "human flourishing."[5] Moreover, narrative ethics is premised on the contextual nature of moral beliefs and practices rooted in the life of a community, and virtue ethics has revived Aristotle's view of moral virtues as functions

4. W. Frankena, "The Naturalistic Fallacy," *Mind* 48 (1939): 464.
5. Hilary Putnam, *Realism with a Human Face* (Harvard Univ. Press, 1990), pt. 2. He shows a more open attitude to theism in the opening pages of his Gifford Lectures, *Renewing Philosophy* (Harvard Univ. Press, 1992), and in his comments on James's *Will to Believe*.

of emotional aspects of human nature. In other words, an intrinsic teleology is at work.[6] Consider also Kant's case in his *Critique of Judgment:* the moral teleology he finds in both the aesthetic possibilities of nature and the moral potential of aesthetic experience must, if mechanistic explanations are only phenomenal, be real, grounded in the thing-in-itself.

I have spoken of value-potential rather than actual value for two reasons. First, the self as valuing being must also meet the conditions needed, for actual aesthetic and moral experience and for human value judgments to occur. Second, nature itself has potential for negative as well as positive value, for discord as well as harmony, ugliness as well as beauty, pain as well as pleasure. Sex has potential for abuse and selfish indulgence as well as genuine love. Work has potential for greed and oppression as well as economic justice. The inherently possible good may be thwarted either by some natural course of events (what Aristotle called "chance") or by morally insensitive or irresponsible agents. Evil is always a parasitical possibility, perverting the good or depriving the potentially good of its actualization. Yet in the Christian tradition, even evil has its place in relation to God's purposes, and hope persists that ultimately the highest good will yet be realized by God acting to achieve his ends.[7]

We are therefore drawn back to the doctrine of creation and the will of God. As Philip Hefner puts it:

> God is the creator and sustainer of all reality, and he holds things together in the patterns of meaning which he has also created. Being and obligation, is and ought, fact and value — all therefore have their origin and meaning in the same God.[8]

3. In the classical Christian tradition, the intelligible and value-oriented nature of creation pointed to the divine Logos, and the Logos doctrine was the theological basis for a developing *theory of universals.* With the rise of nominalism, Logos doctrine was noticeably eclipsed;

6. E.g., James McClendon, Jr., *Ethics* (Abingdon, 1986); R. B. Kruschwitz and R. C. Roberts, *The Virtues* (Wadsworth, 1987). See also A. E. Taylor, *The Faith of a Moralist* (Macmillan, 1932), vol. 1.

7. See A. F. Holmes, *Contours of a World View* (Eerdmans, 1983), ch. 10.

8. In A. R. Peacocke, ed., *The Sciences and Theology in the Twentieth Century* (Univ. of Notre Dame Press, 1981), p. 60.

right reason turned its attention to psychological forces and consequentialist concerns rather than nature's intrinsic value-orientation. But the Logos doctrine and a concomitant theory of universals have long provided a third resource for grounding ethics in reality.

Two main reasons lay behind the rejection of universals by late medieval thinkers: the voluntaristic objection that God was subordinated to their logical necessities; and the needless proliferation of actual entities if universals exist as real immaterial entities. Yet are these objections insurmountable?

Scotus and Ockham regarded the first three commandments of the decalogue as logically necessary, because God is a necessary being, while the other seven are contingent commands because humans are contingent beings. But would real universals exclude all contingencies? Suppose that universals are "real possibilities" rather than actual entities of an immaterial sort, yet not just thought-objects we construct. With various objectively real logical possibilities for this and other possible worlds, God remains free to chose which of them to instantiate in this actual creation and free to keep actualizing their possibilities or not, as he chooses.[9] The contingencies of creation still depend on the will of God. He did not have to create this actual world or this actual kind of human being, nor does he now have to settle for nature's necessities. Moreover, while the reality of such universals does not proliferate actual entities, yet it provides a teleology by grounding ethics in objective possibilities inherent in nature and in human psychology.

Logos theology has further advantages, for it speaks not only to the ordered unity of nature (hence its historic connections with universals), but also to the reliability of human reason. Following Nietzsche, late twentieth-century philosophers historicize human reason, and MacIntyre asks, "Whose Rationality?" But the Logos doctrine suggests that while there may be historical variations, for example, in what counts as rational justification, there remains a generic rationality that still images the divine Logos. This "basic rationality" is evident minimally in the law of noncontradiction, that A cannot both be and not be at the same time or in the same respect. (Hegel never denied

---

9. An approach of this sort is proposed by Nicholas Wolterstorff, *On Universals* (Univ. of Chicago Press, 1973). It also resembles Whitehead's category of "eternal objects."

this: his dialectic of A and non-A refers to different times and/or respects). But the Logos as the principle of ordered unity suggests more; it suggests that rationality is itself an ordering, unifying activity that seeks to see things as the interrelated coherent whole they actually are. The Logos doctrine thus implies that we can neither reject the fact-value relationship, nor be satisfied with the minimalist (let alone a nihilist) approach. It points beyond a mediating moral psychology towards a maximalist position.

4. While universals have appeal for many reasons, their relation to God-concepts and the metaphysics of creation highlights the *holistic nature of worldviews*. Given the "divine command" basis of Christian ethics, for instance, given also the historical tradition in which it developed and the unavoidability of metaphysical and psychological issues involved, it is evident that moral beliefs are in large measure system-dependent — not only in Christian ethics, but by the same token in other ethical traditions as well. So the issue arises of justifying belief of a holistic sort.

The existence of different worldviews, all of them historically dependent, need not by itself imply relativism. Commonalities of a general sort exist across different traditions, and history itself is not without continuity. In fact, as Jeffrey Stout observes, discontinuity is meaningless without the recognition of relatively continuous values, beliefs, and lines of developing inquiry.[10] We observed four general kinds of positions on the fact-value relationship historically, three of them making a continuous tradition of grounding ethics not just in fact but in relation to some God-concept. The latter include Plato and Aristotle (for all their vagueness about God), Augustine and Aquinas, Ockham and the Reformers, Locke and Reid, Kant and Hegel. This continuous line of inquiry, interrupted by Nietzsche, continues to this day. Rorty seems to be right that ethical realism depends on belief in God. Beyond that lie more specific questions about the nature of God, creation, and humanity, questions that give rise to different holistic views.

Both continuities and differences are therefore to be expected. Plato, who first pointed us in a vaguely theistic direction, recognized the difficulty in weighing different theories and gaining certainty on specific questions. His advice bears repeating in our day:

10. Stout, *Ethics After Babel* (Beacon, 1988).

He should persevere until he has achieved one of two things: either he should discover, or be taught the truth about them; or, if this be impossible, I would have him take the best and most irrefragable of human theories, and let this be the raft on which he sails through life — not without risk, as I admit, if he cannot find some word of God which will more surely and safely carry him.[11]

Plato's reference to "some word of God" may seem to anticipate Duns Scotus's and William of Ockham's attention to the decalogue or the Reformers' appeal to Scripture. But its more immediate historical continuity is with earlier claims that a divine Word ordered the creation and formed human rationality in his own image (this is what ultimately overcomes moral scepticism and anti-realism), and that this Word became incarnate, full of virtues of grace and truth. That this is who captured Mill's moral imagination reminds us not only that common moral beliefs occur in very different holistic views, but also that the justification of moral beliefs may not conform to Enlightenment standards. But that is beyond the scope of this book.

11. *Phaedo*, 85.

Index

Printed in the United States
98229LV00009B/148-162/A

9 780802 843128